Essential Mathematics for Life
Percents, Graphs, and Measurement

Authors

Mary S. Charuhas
Field Representative
Northern Area
Adult Education Service Center
Chicago, IL

The Mathematics Faculty
American Preparatory Institute
Killeen, TX

Valjean McLenighan
Educational Consultant and Writer
Chicago, IL

Dorothy Davis McMurtry
Assistant to the President
Chicago Urban Skills Institute
City Colleges of Chicago
Chicago, IL

Academic Editor

Dr. Violet M. Malone
Past President
Adult Education Association of the USA
(now AAACE)
Chairperson
National Coalition for Literacy
Professor and State Leader
Extension Education
University of Illinois at Urbana-Champaign
Urbana-Champaign, IL

General Advisor

Dr. Alan B. Knox
President
American Association for
Adult and Continuing Education (AAACE)
Professor of Continuing Education
University of Wisconsin-Madison
Madison, WI

Advisory Board

Noe B. Calvillo
Director
Hidalgo-Starr Cooperative
for Adult and Community
Education Programs
Prime Sponsor
McAllen Independent School District
McAllen, TX

Norman B. Carr
Educational Consultant and
Former Education Director
U.S. Army Forces Command
Daytona Beach, FL

Katharine Kharas
Instructor of Mathematics
Mesa College
San Diego Community
College District
San Diego, CA

Mary Gant Turner
President
Turner Associates
Washington, DC
Former Assistant Superintendent
Adult and Continuing Education
Public Schools of the District
of Columbia

Lifelong Learning Division
Scott, Foresman and Company

1900 East Lake Avenue
Glenview, IL 60025
1-800-323-5482
1-800-323-9501 (Illinois)
1-312-729-3000 (Alaska & Hawaii residents)

Contents

ISBN: 0-673-24018-5

Copyright © 1985, 1981
Scott, Foresman and Company.
All Rights Reserved.
Printed in the United States
of America.
345678910-DAN-93929190898786

Photo credits
All photographs are the property
of Scott, Foresman.

Part 2 Proportion, graphs, and measurement

Percents

95% natural (wood, glass, paper)

5% synthetic (ink)

93% natural (straw)

7% synthetic (plastic)

75% natural (down, metal)

25% synthetic (nylon)

98% natural (cotton)

2% synthetic (plastic)

100% natural (leather, silver)

100% natural (cotton, metal)

20% natural (metal)

80% synthetic (plastic, foam rubber)

100% synthetic

75% natural (metal, leather)

25% synthetic rubber

5% natural (jute)

95% synthetic (polyester)

1

Lesson 1
Adding and subtracting decimals

Rules:
    1. Write the numbers in columns. Line up the decimal points.
    2. Remember whole numbers have a decimal point at the right.
    3. Add zeros to the right of the decimal point if needed.

A.
$1 + 2.87 =$

$$\begin{array}{r} 1.00 \\ +2.87 \\ \hline 3.87 \end{array}$$

B.
$.08 + .93 =$

$$\begin{array}{r} .08 \\ +.93 \\ \hline 1.01 \end{array}$$

C.
$7 - 1.543 =$

$$\begin{array}{r} 7.000 \\ -1.543 \\ \hline 5.457 \end{array}$$

D.
$12.09 - .003 =$

$$\begin{array}{r} 12.090 \\ -\ \ .003 \\ \hline 12.087 \end{array}$$

Add or subtract.

1. $10 - 1.37 =$ _____

2. $2.44 - .76 =$ _____

3. $11.28 - .12 =$ _____

4. $1044.3 - 257.07 =$ _____

5. $.99 - .9 =$ _____

6. $454.008 + 5.12 + .063 =$ _____

7. $1001.1 + 1.9 + 20.05 =$ _____

8. $565 + .25 + 1.78 =$ _____

9. $5.54 + 10 + 1.003 =$ _____

10. $956 + 77 + .88 =$ _____

Objective/Add and subtract decimals.

0   8 10

Lesson 2
Multiplying decimals

Rules:
1. Multiply as usual.
2. Count the number of decimal places in both numbers. Add to find the total.
3. Use the total to count off decimal places in the answer. Count from right to left.
4. Fill in with zeros if more decimal places are needed.

A.

30	0 place
×2.3	+1 place
69.0	1 place

B.

1.078	3 places
× .003	+3 places
.003234	6 places

C.

.003	3 places
× .06	+2 places
.00018	5 places

Multiply.

1. 453
    × .03

4. 5751
    × .006

7. 2981
    × .011

10. .025
     ×   22

2. 23.54
    ×   .05

5. 45.67
    ×   .23

8. 555
    × 1.76

11. 950
     × .087

3. 11.1
    × .203

6. 2591
    × .8902

9. 178.6
    × .905

12. 1.155
     × .8321

Lesson 3
Decimal division

Rules for dividing decimals by whole numbers:
1. Divide as usual.
2. Bring the decimal point straight up into the answer.

A.
$$\begin{array}{r} 2.1 \\ 2\overline{)4.2} \\ \underline{4} \\ 2 \\ \underline{2} \end{array}$$

B.
$$\begin{array}{r} .125 \\ 8\overline{)1.000} \\ \underline{8} \\ 20 \\ \underline{16} \\ 40 \\ \underline{40} \end{array}$$

Rules for dividing decimals by decimals:
1. Move the decimal point in the divisor all the way to the right.
2. Move the decimal point in the dividend the same number of decimal places to the right.
3. Fill in empty decimal places with zeros.
4. Bring the decimal point straight up into the answer.

C.
$$\begin{array}{r} .6 \\ 6.\overline{)\,.3.6} \\ \underline{3\ 6} \end{array}$$

D.
$.2 \div .04 = ?$
$$\begin{array}{r} 5. \\ 04.\overline{)\,20.} \\ \underline{20} \end{array}$$

Divide.

1. $.5\overline{)3\ 0\ 0}$ _____

2. $8\overline{)6\ 4\ .\ 8}$ _____

3. $.04\overline{)1\ .\ 6}$ _____

4. $45\overline{)3\ .\ 9\ 1\ 5}$ _____

5. $55 \div .11 =$ _____

6. $.25\overline{)7}$ _____

7. $1.6\overline{)\,.\ 7\ 2}$ _____

8. $.005\overline{)\,.\ 2\ 5}$ _____

9. $32\overline{)7\ .\ 3\ 9\ 2}$ _____

10. $9.9 \div .033 =$ _____

11. $.003\overline{)2}$ _____

12. $.009\overline{)6\ 3\ .\ 9}$ _____

13. $.08\overline{)5\ .\ 6}$ _____

14. $253\overline{)2\ 8\ .\ 9\ 6\ 8\ 5}$ _____

15. $.51 \div .017 =$ _____

Objective/Divide decimals.

0   12   15

Rule for reducing a fraction:
  Divide the numerator and the
  denominator by the same number.

$$\frac{5}{25} = \frac{5 \div 5}{25 \div 5} = \frac{1}{5}$$

Reduce.

1. $\frac{6}{72} =$ _____

2. $8\frac{7}{28} =$ _____

3. $11\frac{25}{50} =$ _____

4. $\frac{10}{200} =$ _____

5. $10\frac{22}{33} =$ _____

6. $17\frac{3}{9} =$ _____

Rules for writing equivalent fractions:
  1. Divide the smaller denominator
     into the larger denominator.
  2. Multiply the numerator by the
     answer to find the missing numerator.

$$\frac{2}{3} = \frac{}{18} \qquad 18 \div 3 = 6$$

$$\frac{2 \times 6}{3 \times 6} = \frac{12}{18}$$

Write equivalent fractions.

7. $\frac{3}{5} = \frac{}{25}$

8. $\frac{1}{9} = \frac{}{81}$

9. $\frac{9}{11} = \frac{}{55}$

10. $\frac{7}{8} = \frac{}{56}$

11. $\frac{5}{6} = \frac{}{72}$

12. $\frac{2}{13} = \frac{}{39}$

Rules for finding a common denominator
(choose one.):
  1. Use one of the denominators
     given if the other denominators
     divide evenly into it.

     $\frac{1}{24}$ $\frac{1}{12}$ 12 divides evenly into 24.
                24 is the common denominator.

  2. Multiply the denominators together
     to get a common denominator.

     $\frac{1}{6}$ $\frac{1}{4}$ 6 × 4 = 24
              24 is the common denominator.

  3. Multiply two or more of the
     denominators together to get a
     common denominator.

     $\frac{1}{8}$ $\frac{1}{3}$ $\frac{1}{2}$ 8 × 3 = 24, and
                2 divides evenly into 24.
                24 is the common denominator.

Find a common denominator.

13. $\frac{2}{3}$ $\frac{1}{9}$ _____

14. $\frac{1}{2}$ $\frac{1}{4}$ $\frac{1}{5}$ _____

15. $\frac{7}{8}$ $\frac{3}{16}$ _____

16. $\frac{2}{3}$ $\frac{3}{4}$ $\frac{4}{5}$ _____

17. $\frac{5}{9}$ $\frac{1}{2}$ _____

18. $\frac{11}{12}$ $\frac{1}{5}$ $\frac{2}{30}$ _____

Objective/Understand fractions.

Rules for renaming mixed numbers:
1. Rename the whole number as a mixed number. Use the same denominator as in the given fraction.
2. Add the fractions.

$$7\frac{1}{4} = 6 + 1 + \frac{1}{4}$$
$$= 6 + \frac{4}{4} + \frac{1}{4}$$
$$= 6\frac{5}{4}$$

Rename these mixed numbers.

19. $9\frac{1}{2} = 8\frac{}{2}$ 22. $6 = 5\frac{}{3}$

20. $9 = 8\frac{}{12}$ 23. $21\frac{7}{8} = 20\frac{}{8}$

21. $47\frac{3}{8} = 46\frac{}{8}$ 24. $19\frac{1}{2} = 18\frac{}{2}$

Rules for changing fractions to mixed numbers:
1. Divide the numerator by the denominator.
2. Write the remainder as a fraction.

$$\frac{15}{7} = 7\overline{)15} = 2\frac{1}{7}$$
$$\phantom{\frac{15}{7} = 7)}\underline{14}$$
$$\phantom{\frac{15}{7} = 7)}1R$$

Change these to mixed or whole numbers.

25. $\frac{22}{5} =$ _____   28. $\frac{20}{20} =$ _____

26. $\frac{30}{4} =$ _____   29. $\frac{48}{9} =$ _____

27. $\frac{99}{11} =$ _____   30. $\frac{36}{36} =$ _____

Rules for changing mixed numbers to improper fractions:
1. Multiply the denominator by the whole number. Add the numerator.
2. Write the result over the original denominator.

$3\frac{1}{4}$ ← numerator
$\phantom{3\frac{1}{4}}$ ← denominator

$$4 \times 3 + 1 = 13$$

$$3\frac{1}{4} = \frac{13}{4}$$

Change these to improper fractions.

31. $5\frac{2}{5} =$ _____   34. $9\frac{2}{3} =$ _____

32. $33\frac{1}{3} =$ _____   35. $16\frac{2}{3} =$ _____

33. $7\frac{3}{8} =$ _____   36. $8\frac{1}{3} =$ _____

Objective/Understand fractions.

0   29   36

Lesson 5
Adding and subtracting fractions

Rules:
1. Find a common denominator for the fractions.
2. Add or subtract the numerators of the fractions.
    Add or subtract the whole numbers.
3. If the top fraction in a subtraction problem is less
    than the bottom fraction, rename the top whole number.
4. Reduce all answers.

Study these examples.

A.

$$\begin{array}{r} 1\frac{3}{5} \\ -\ \ \frac{2}{5} \\ \hline 1\frac{1}{5} \end{array}$$

B.

$$\begin{array}{r} 4\frac{2}{3} = 4\frac{8}{12} \\ +\ 3\frac{1}{4} = 3\frac{3}{12} \\ \hline 7\frac{11}{12} \end{array}$$

C.

$$\begin{array}{r} 5\frac{3}{10} = 5\frac{3}{10} \\ 6\frac{4}{5} = 6\frac{8}{10} \\ +\ 1\frac{1}{2} = 1\frac{5}{10} \\ \hline 12\frac{16}{10} = 13\frac{6}{10} = 13\frac{3}{5} \end{array}$$

D.

$$\begin{array}{r} 7 \\ -\ \frac{2}{7} \end{array}$$

$\frac{2}{7}$ cannot be subtracted from a whole number.

Rename the 7 so it is a mixed number. For the denominator of the new fraction, choose the denominator of $\frac{2}{7}$.

$7 = 6 + \frac{7}{7}$

$$\begin{array}{r} \overset{6}{7}\frac{7}{7} \\ -\ \ \frac{2}{7} \\ \hline 6\frac{5}{7} \end{array}$$

E.

$$\begin{array}{r} 5\frac{1}{3} = 5\frac{8}{24} \\ -\ \ \frac{3}{8} = \ \ \frac{9}{24} \end{array}$$

Find a common denominator.
9 cannot be subtracted from 8.

Rename the 5 as a mixed number, using the common denominator.

$5 = 4 + \frac{24}{24}$

$$\overset{4}{5}\frac{8}{24} + \frac{24}{24}$$
$$-\ \ \frac{9}{24}$$

Add $4 + \frac{24}{24}$ to $\frac{8}{24}$.

$4 + \frac{24}{24} + \frac{8}{24} = 4 + \frac{32}{24}$

$$\begin{array}{r} 4\frac{32}{24} \\ -\ \ \frac{9}{24} \\ \hline 4\frac{23}{24} \end{array}$$

Now subtract.

Add or subtract.

1. $1\frac{3}{10}$
   $+\ 2\frac{3}{10}$

2. $1\ 7\frac{23}{40}$
   $-\ \ \ 5\frac{11}{40}$

3. $1\ 5\frac{1}{3}$
   $-\ \ \ 1\frac{3}{4}$

4. $17\frac{8}{11} + 10\frac{2}{3} = $ _____

5. $10\frac{3}{4} - \frac{1}{3} = $ _____

6. $95\frac{3}{4} - 42\frac{5}{6} = $ _____

7. $1\ 2$
   $-\ \ \ \frac{2}{3}$

8. $2\frac{4}{9}$
   $+\ \ \frac{5}{9}$

9. $7\frac{7}{8}$
   $+\ 6$

10. $9\frac{1}{2} + 7\frac{1}{2} = $ _____

11. $28\frac{8}{9} - 8\frac{7}{8} = $ _____

12. $6\frac{3}{5} + 1\frac{2}{7} = $ _____

13. 6
    $-\ \ \frac{5}{8}$

14. $1\ 4\frac{4}{7}$
    $+\ \ \ 2\frac{4}{5}$

15. $2\ 3\frac{2}{11}$
    $-\ \ \ 1\frac{4}{33}$

16. $13\frac{2}{3} - \frac{2}{3} = $ _____

17. $13\frac{5}{11} + 5\frac{1}{3} = $ _____

18. $17\frac{23}{40} - 8\frac{11}{40} = $ _____

Circle the letter of the right answer.

19. Last week Vince worked $9\frac{2}{3}$ hours overtime. This week he worked $7\frac{1}{6}$ hours overtime. How much overtime did Vince work in all?

   a. $17\frac{5}{6}$ hours   c. $16\frac{5}{6}$ hours

   b. $16\frac{1}{2}$ hours   d. 17 hours

20. How many more hours did Vince work last week than this week?

   a. $2\frac{1}{2}$ hours   c. $2\frac{1}{6}$ hours

   b. $9\frac{2}{3}$ hours   d. 2 hours

8

0   16   20

Lesson 6
Multiplying fractions

Rules:
1. Change all mixed numbers to improper fractions.
2. Cancel if possible.
3. Multiply straight across.
4. Reduce.

Study these examples.

A.

$\frac{3}{4} \times \frac{1}{2} = \frac{3}{8}$ Multiply straight across.

B.

$\frac{\cancel{3}^1}{\cancel{7}_1} \times \frac{\cancel{7}^1}{\cancel{9}_3} = \frac{1}{3}$ Cancel.
Multiply straight across.

C.

$1\frac{1}{3} \times 4\frac{5}{8}$

$= \frac{4}{3} \times \frac{37}{8}$ Change mixed numbers to improper fractions.

$= \frac{\cancel{4}^1}{3} \times \frac{37}{\cancel{8}_2}$ Cancel.

$= \frac{37}{6}$ Multiply straight across.

$= 6\frac{1}{6}$ Reduce.

Multiply.

1. $\frac{1}{2} \times \frac{1}{3} =$ _____

2. $1\frac{1}{2} \times \frac{8}{9} =$ _____

3. $\frac{2}{5} \times \frac{5}{12} \times \frac{8}{13} =$ _____

4. $25 \times \frac{1}{8} =$ _____

5. $8\frac{1}{3} \times 4\frac{3}{5} \times \frac{15}{46} =$ _____

6. $\frac{5}{8} \times \frac{7}{25} =$ _____

7. $5\frac{2}{5} \times 3\frac{1}{3} =$ _____

8. $\frac{5}{8} \times 4 \times \frac{16}{25} =$ _____

9. $93 \times 1\frac{1}{3} =$ _____

10. $11\frac{1}{9} \times \frac{9}{100} \times 9\frac{3}{8} =$ _____

11. $63 \times 7\frac{1}{7} =$ _____

12. $13\frac{1}{5} \times 4\frac{1}{11} \times 2\frac{1}{2} =$ _____

Lesson 7
Dividing by fractions

Rules for dividing by fractions:
1. Change all mixed numbers to improper fractions.
2. Invert the divisor.
3. Cancel if possible.
4. Multiply straight across.
5. Reduce.

Study these examples.

A.

$$\frac{1}{2} \div \frac{3}{8} = \frac{1}{\underset{1}{2}} \times \frac{\overset{4}{8}}{3} = \frac{4}{3} = 1\frac{1}{3}$$

B.

$$2\frac{1}{3} \div 3\frac{5}{6} = \frac{7}{3} \div \frac{23}{6} = \frac{7}{\underset{1}{3}} \times \frac{\overset{2}{6}}{23} = \frac{14}{23}$$

Divide.

1. $\frac{1}{8} \div \frac{1}{8} =$ _____

2. $22 \div \frac{1}{2} =$ _____

3. $6\frac{3}{4} \div 9 =$ _____

4. $\frac{7}{8} \div 1\frac{5}{16} =$ _____

5. $\frac{2}{3} \div \frac{4}{9} =$ _____

6. $15 \div \frac{3}{4} =$ _____

7. $\frac{2}{5} \div 1\frac{3}{5} =$ _____

8. $5\frac{2}{9} \div \frac{1}{27} =$ _____

9. $\frac{11}{12} \div \frac{3}{4} =$ _____

10. $2\frac{3}{8} \div 19 =$ _____

11. $8\frac{1}{4} \div \frac{11}{20} =$ _____

12. $1\frac{1}{2} \div \frac{3}{4} =$ _____

Objective/Divide fractions.

0   10   12

Lesson 8
Writing equal decimals and fractions

Rules for writing fractions as decimals:
1. Fractions mean division. Divide the numerator by the denominator.
2. Use a decimal point and zeros if needed.
3. Carry out to 2 decimal places. Make any remainder a fraction.

A.

$\frac{1}{2}$ means $2\overline{\smash{)}1.0}$ .5
$\underline{1.0}$

B.

$3\frac{1}{3} = \frac{10}{3}$ means $3\overline{\smash{)}10.00}$ $3.33\frac{1}{3}$
$\underline{9}$
$1\;0$
$\underline{9}$
10
$\underline{9}$
$1R$

Remember, "equivalent fraction" is another way to say "equal fraction."

Rules for writing decimals as fractions:
1. Draw a line under the decimal.
2. Put a zero under every number.
3. Write 1 for the decimal point.
4. Drop the decimal point and reduce.

C.
$.358 \rightarrow \frac{358}{1000}$ becomes $\frac{358}{1000} = \frac{179}{500}$

D.
$1.005 \rightarrow 1\frac{005}{1000} \rightarrow 1\frac{5}{1000} = 1\frac{1}{200}$

Write as decimals.

1. $\frac{1}{10}$ _____

2. $1\frac{1}{2}$ _____

3. $\frac{1}{6}$ _____

4. $\frac{2}{5}$ _____

5. $5\frac{3}{8}$ _____

6. $\frac{2}{3}$ _____

7. $\frac{3}{4}$ _____

8. $11\frac{9}{10}$ _____

Write as fractions.

9. .125 _____

10. .25 _____

11. 5.01 _____

12. .2 _____

13. .85 _____

14. 6.125 _____

15. .0012 _____

16. .003 _____

Lesson 9
Comparing decimals and fractions

Which is larger, $\frac{1}{10}$ or .003?

Fraction method:
1. Write both numbers as fractions using a common denominator.
2. Compare numerators.

$$\frac{1}{10} = \frac{100}{1000}$$

$$.003 = \frac{3}{1000}$$

$\frac{1}{10}$ is larger,

or $\frac{1}{10} > .003$.

Decimal method:
1. Write both numbers as decimals.
2. Line up the decimal points.
3. Fill in zeros as placeholders.
4. Compare numbers.

$$\frac{1}{10} \;= .1 \;= .100$$

$$.003 = .003$$

$\frac{1}{10}$ is greater.

Which is larger?

1. $\frac{3}{4}$ or .5

2. .3 or $\frac{1}{4}$

3. $\frac{8}{9}$ or 1.1

4. .85 or $\frac{5}{6}$

5. $\frac{1}{3}$ or .4

Which is smaller?

6. $\frac{1}{10}$ or .09

7. .009 or $\frac{3}{100}$

8. $\frac{3}{4}$ or .49

9. $2\frac{4}{5}$ or 3.01

10. $\frac{1}{8}$ or .2

Put in order from the smallest to the largest.

11. .09   .9 $\frac{1}{5}$

12. $\frac{3}{8}$ $\frac{5}{9}$ .6

Objective/Compare decimals and fractions.

Pretest/Unit 2
Meaning of percent

1. What percent of the squares are green? _____

2. What percent of the squares are white? _____

3. What percent of the box has squares? _____

Change to decimals.

4. 25% = _____   5. 245% = _____   6. 1% = _____

7. $66\frac{2}{3}\% =$ _____   8. 77% = _____   9. .08% = _____

Change to fractions.

10. 90% = _____   11. $16\frac{2}{3}\% =$ _____   12. 288% = _____

13. 68% = _____   14. $\frac{1}{2}\% =$ _____   15. 4% = _____

Change to percents.

16. $.33\frac{1}{3} =$ _____   17. $1\frac{3}{4} =$ _____   18. 42.1 = _____

19. 1 = _____   20. .0082 = _____   21. $\frac{1}{5} =$ _____

Write in order from the smallest to the largest.

22. $\frac{1}{4}$ .75 $\frac{4}{5}$ 30%   _____ _____ _____ _____

23. .33 $\frac{1}{6}$ $\frac{5}{8}$ 15%   _____ _____ _____ _____

24. .04   18%   2   2.1   _____ _____ _____ _____

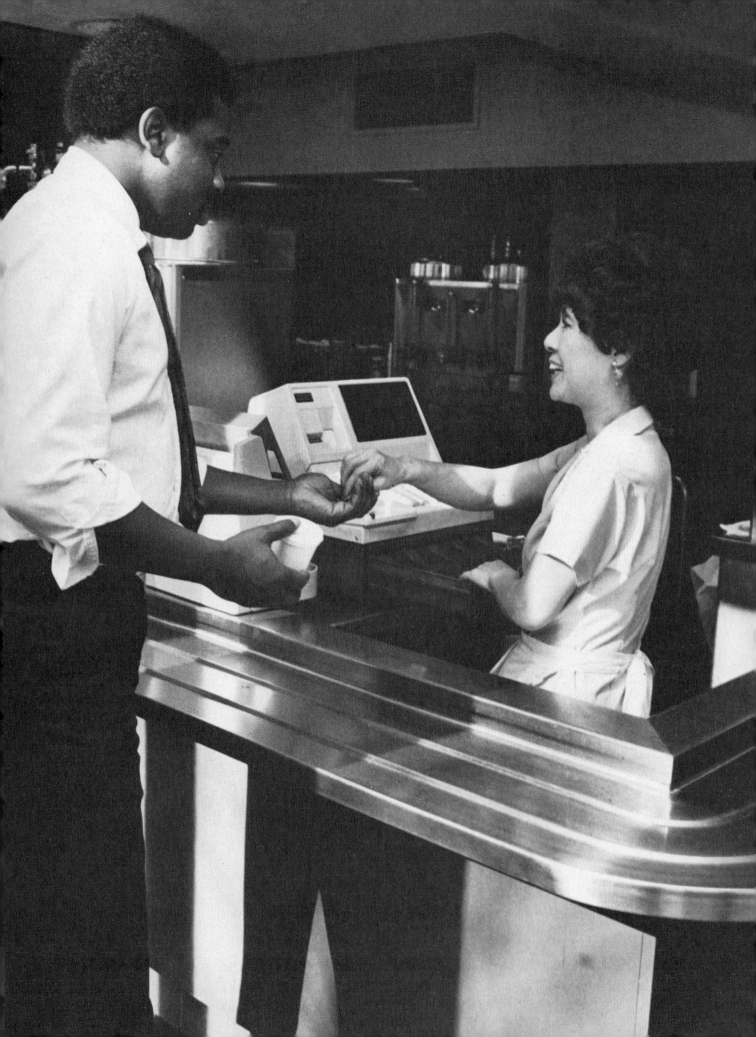

Lesson 10
Recognizing percents

Divide a whole unit into 100 equal parts.
One percent is one part out of the 100 parts.
All 100 parts together are 100%.

Percent means based on 100 parts.
The symbol for percent is %.

A.

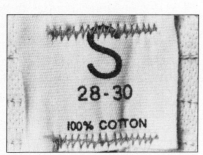

The whole unit is a T-shirt. The label says 100% cotton. It means that only cotton was used to make the T-shirt.

B.

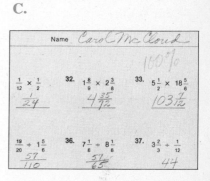

The whole unit is a bottle of corn oil. The label says 100% corn oil. It means that the only ingredient in the bottle is corn oil.

C.

The whole unit is all the questions on the test. The grade of 100% means that all the answers are correct.

Percents are like our money system.
One dollar is like one whole unit.

Divide one dollar into 100 parts.

Divide one whole unit into 100 parts.

One dollar equals 100 cents.
$1.00 = 100¢

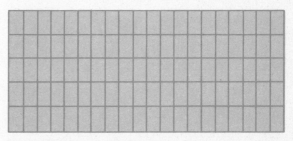

One whole unit equals 100 percent.
1 whole unit = 100%

Answer the questions below each picture.

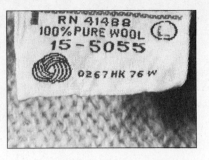

1. a. What is the whole unit?

_____

b. What does 100% natural mean?

_____

2. a. What is the whole unit?

_____

b. What does 100% pure wool mean?

_____

3. a. What is the whole unit?

_____

b. What does it mean to spend 100% of a dollar?

_____

Answer the questions below.

4. What percent of the dollar is shaded?

_____

5. What percent of the month is marked off?

July						
	1	2	3	4	5	6
7	8	9	10	11	12	13
14	15	16	17	18	19	20
21	22	23	24	25	26	27
28	29	30	31			

_____

6. What percent of the committee voted YES?

Vote of building committee		
	Yes	**No**
Anderson	×	
Klein	×	
O'Brien	×	
Pereg	×	

_____

7. The sign on the theater's ticket window read "sold out." What percent of the evening's tickets were sold?

_____

Objective/Recognize percents.

0   6   7

Lesson 11
What percents mean

Less than 100% means less than one whole unit.
This penny is less than one dollar.

1¢ < $1.00

1¢
1¢ equals $\frac{1}{100}$ of a dollar.

The percent shaded < one whole unit.

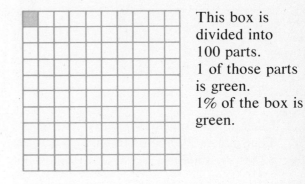

This box is divided into 100 parts.
1 of those parts is green.
1% of the box is green.

1%
1% equals $\frac{1}{100}$ of a whole unit.

Answer the questions about each picture.
The first is done as an example.

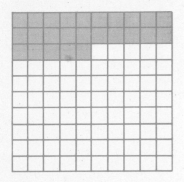

This box is divided into 100 parts.

25 parts are green.

75 parts are white.

What percent of the box is green?
   Answer: 25% is green, because each of the green parts equals 1%.

What percent of the box is white?
   Answer: 75% is white, because each white part equals 1%.

What percent does the whole box represent?
   Answer: 100%, because the whole unit always equals 100%.

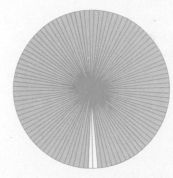

This circle divided into 100 parts.

98 parts are green.

2 parts are white.

1. What percent of the circle is green? _____

2. What percent of the circle is white? _____

3. What percent does the whole circle represent? _____

More than 100% means more than one whole unit.

Two dollars are like two whole units.

Each dollar equals 100 cents.
That makes 200 cents in all.
$2.00 = 200¢

Each unit is divided into 100 parts.
That makes 200 parts in all.
2 whole units = 200%.

Answer the questions.

Each box is divided into 100 parts.
100 parts of Box 1 are green.
68 parts of Box 2 are green.

4. What percent of Box 1
    is green?   _____

5. What percent of Box 2
    is green?   _____

6. Altogether, what percent
    is green?   _____

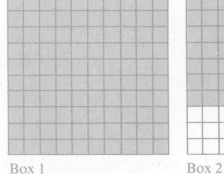

Box 1   Box 2

Each triangle is divided into 100 parts.
100 parts of Triangle 1 are green.
4 parts of Triangle 2 are green.

7. What percent of Triangle 1
    is green?   _____

8. What percent of Triangle 2
    is green?   _____

9. Altogether, what percent is
    green?   _____

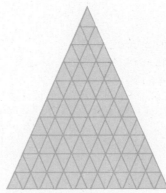

Triangle 1   Triangle 2

Objective/Understand percents.

Less than 1% means less than $\frac{1}{100}$ of a whole unit.

Half a cent
is like
half a
percent.

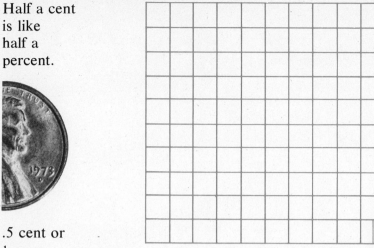

.5 cent or
$\frac{1}{2}$ cent

This box is divided into
100 parts.

$99\frac{1}{2}$ of the parts are white.

$\frac{1}{2}$ of one of the parts is green.

The green section is

$\frac{1}{2}$% or .5% or $\frac{\frac{1}{2}}{100}$.

Answer the questions.

This box is divided into 100 parts.
$99\frac{1}{4}$ of the parts are white.
$\frac{3}{4}$ of one of the parts is green.

10. What percent of the box is
    white? _____

11. What percent of the box is
    green? _____

12. What percent does the whole
    box represent? _____

13. Define **100%** in your own words.

    _____

    _____

14. Define **less than 100%** in your own words.

    _____

    _____

15. Define **less than 1%** in your own words.

    _____

    _____

16. Define **more than 100%** in your own words.

    _____

    _____

For extra practice see page 136.

0   13   16

Objective/Understand percents.

19

Using nutritional information from labels

Angela wanted to make sure she was getting 100% of the recommended daily allowance (RDA) of iron. She started by checking the nutritional information on the labels of the food she bought. The labels give the percent of the RDA in one serving of the food.

Here is the chart Angela made.

One serving	% RDA iron
Prune juice	15
Hot farina cereal	45
Cold cereal	20
Natural wheat bread	10
White bread	4
Beans	25
Spaghetti	10
Rice pudding	5

Here is what she decided to eat in one day.

These foods	% RDA iron
Prune juice	15
Hot farina cereal	45
Natural wheat bread	10
Beans	25
Rice pudding	5
Adding all the percents, Angela came up with a total of 100%.	100%

What would you eat to get 100% of the RDA of calcium? Use the information below. Make your list and be sure the percents add up to 100%.

One serving	% RDA calcium	These foods	% RDA calcium
Cold cereal with milk	20	_____	_____
Yogurt	30	_____	_____
Ice cream	30	_____	_____
Swiss cheese	25	_____	_____
Pudding	15	_____	_____
Cream of tomato soup	15	_____	_____
Beans	15	_____	_____
		Total	_____

Lesson 12
Writing equal fractions, decimals, and percents

Fractions, decimals, and percents are different ways of writing the same value.

Percents are a common way of talking about money, interest, taxes, loans, and payroll withholding. However, you cannot multiply or divide by percents.

Before you can solve percent problems you must change the percent to a decimal or a fraction.

Here are different ways **one quarter** can be written.

$25¢ = \$.25 = \frac{1}{4}$ dollar

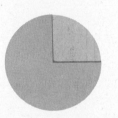

$$\frac{1}{4} \quad = \quad .25 \quad = \quad 25\%$$

fraction   decimal   percent

Write the answers.

1. Write half a dollar as a fraction.

5. Write a dime as a fraction.

2. Write half a dollar with a ¢ sign.

6. Write a dime with a ¢ sign.

3. Write half a dollar with a $ sign.

7. Write a dime with a $ sign.

4. If one-half of the 100 people working in a factory have a savings plan, what percent would that be?

8. Three-fourths of the cars that came into a gas station used unleaded gasoline. What percent would that be?

Objective/Write equal fractions, decimals, and percents.

0   6   8

Lesson 13

Changing percents to decimals

Rules:
1. Drop the percent sign.
2. Divide by 100.

A.

$$22\% = 100\overline{)22.00} = .22$$

with $.22$ above the division.

Shortcut:
1. Drop the percent sign.
2. Move the decimal point two places to the left.
   Fractions at the end of a percent do not count as a decimal place.

B.
$$22\% = .22. = .22$$

C.
$$247\% = 2.47. = 2.47$$

D.
$$.3\% = .00.3 = .003$$

E.
$$8\tfrac{1}{3}\% = .08\tfrac{1}{3} = .08\tfrac{1}{3}$$

Change these percents to decimals.

1. $67\% =$ _____

2. $198\% =$ _____

3. $2\% =$ _____

4. $59\% =$ _____

5. $999\% =$ _____

6. $16\tfrac{2}{3}\% =$ _____

7. $.5\% =$ _____

8. $45.6\% =$ _____

9. $37.08\% =$ _____

10. $.076\% =$ _____

11. $12\tfrac{1}{2}\% =$ _____

12. $44\% =$ _____

13. $7\% =$ _____

14. $33\tfrac{1}{3}\% =$ _____

15. $8\tfrac{1}{7}\% =$ _____

Write the percent as a decimal.

16. the 5% of Joe's pay that is withheld for medical insurance _____

17. the 150% increase in the price of bread over the past two years _____

Objective/Change percents to decimals.

Lesson 14
Changing decimals to percents

Rules:
1. Multiply the decimal by 100.
2. Add the percent sign.

$$
\begin{array}{r}
.75 \\
\times \ 100 \\
\hline
75.00 = 75\%
\end{array}
$$

Shortcut:
1. Move the decimal point two places to the right.
2. Add the percent sign.
   Fractions at the end of a decimal do not count as a decimal place.

A.
.75 = .75.% = 75%

B.
5 = 5.00.% = 500%

C.
.0025 = .00.25% = .25%

D.
$.83\frac{1}{3}$ = $.83.\frac{1}{3}\%$ = $83\frac{1}{3}\%$

Change these decimals to percents.

1. .35 = _____

2. .01 = _____

3. 9 = _____

4. .002 = _____

5. $.33\frac{1}{3}$ = _____

6. .9 = _____

7. 1.25 = _____

8. 1 = _____

9. .1 = _____

10. $.16\frac{2}{3}$ = _____

11. .55 = _____

12. .8 = _____

13. 2.5 = _____

14. .006 = _____

15. $.08\frac{1}{2}$ = _____

Write the decimal as a percent.

16. a .005 increase in gasoline taxes _____

17. Gasohol is .8 alcohol. What percent of it is alcohol? _____

Objective/Change decimals to percents.

0   14   17

Lesson 15
Changing percents to fractions

Rules:
1. Write the percent amount as a fraction. Drop the percent sign.
2. Multiply by $\frac{1}{100}$.
3. Reduce.

A.

$$8\% = \frac{8}{1} \times \frac{1}{100} = \frac{8}{100} = \frac{2}{25}$$

B.

$$972\% = \frac{\overset{243}{972}}{1} \times \frac{1}{\underset{25}{100}} = \frac{243}{25} = 9\frac{18}{25}$$

C.

$$\frac{1}{2}\% = \frac{1}{2} \times \frac{1}{100} = \frac{1}{200}$$

D.

$$12\frac{1}{2}\% = \frac{25}{2} \times \frac{1}{\underset{4}{100}} = \frac{1}{8}$$

Change these percents to fractions.

1. $90\% = $ _____

2. $775\% = $ _____

3. $33\frac{1}{3}\% = $ _____

4. $100\% = $ _____

5. $190\% = $ _____

6. $87\frac{1}{2}\% = $ _____

7. $22\% = $ _____

8. $166\frac{2}{3}\% = $ _____

9. $31\frac{2}{3}\% = $ _____

10. $60\% = $ _____

11. $150\% = $ _____

12. $16\frac{2}{3}\% = $ _____

13. $85\% = $ _____

14. $265\% = $ _____

15. $83\frac{1}{3}\% = $ _____

Write the percent as a fraction.

16. Tables are on sale for 25% off. What fraction off is this? _____

17. Ground beef is marked 70% lean. What fraction is lean? _____

0　　　　14　　17

Lesson 16
Changing fractions to percents

Rules:
1. Multiply by $\frac{100}{1}$.
2. Reduce.
3. Add the percent sign.

A.

$$\frac{1}{2} = \left(\frac{1}{\overset{1}{\underset{1}{2}}} \times \frac{\overset{50}{\cancel{100}}}{1}\right)\% = 50\%$$

B.

$$\frac{1}{500} = \left(\frac{1}{\underset{5}{\cancel{500}}} \times \frac{\overset{1}{\cancel{100}}}{1}\right)\% = \frac{1}{5}\%$$

Change mixed numbers to improper fractions before multiplying.

C.

$$2\frac{1}{3} = \left(\frac{7}{3} \times \frac{100}{1}\right)\% = \frac{700}{3}\% = 233\frac{1}{3}\%$$

Change these fractions to percents.

1. $\frac{2}{5} =$ _____

2. $\frac{1}{4} =$ _____

3. $\frac{1}{25} =$ _____

4. $\frac{4}{9} =$ _____

5. $2\frac{9}{10} =$ _____

6. $\frac{1}{50} =$ _____

7. $\frac{33}{1000} =$ _____

8. $\frac{1}{30} =$ _____

9. $1\frac{3}{4} =$ _____

10. $\frac{7}{8} =$ _____

11. $\frac{67}{500} =$ _____

12. $5\frac{1}{4} =$ _____

Write the fraction as a percent.

13. a $\frac{1}{6}$ decrease in the crime rate of big cities _____

14. the $\frac{1}{12}$ of the men in the United States who are color-blind _____

Objective/Change fractions to percents.

0   11   14

Lesson 17
Comparing fractions, decimals, and percents

Fractions, decimals, and percents are three ways to write the same value.

To compare fractions, decimals, and percents, change them all to fractions or all to decimals.

Compare .77, $\frac{7}{9}$, and .9%.
Write them in order from smallest to largest.

<table>
<tr><td>Fraction method</td><td>Decimal method</td></tr>
<tr><td>$.77 = \frac{77}{100} = \frac{6930}{9000}$</td><td>$.77 = .770$</td></tr>
<tr><td>$\frac{7}{9} = \frac{7000}{9000}$</td><td>$\frac{7}{9} = 9\overline{)7.000}^{\,.777\frac{7}{9}} = .777\frac{7}{9}$</td></tr>
<tr><td>$.9\% = \frac{9}{1000} = \frac{81}{9000}$</td><td>$.9\% = .009$</td></tr>
<tr><td>Compare the numerators.</td><td>Compare place value.</td></tr>
<tr><td>$\frac{81}{9000}, \frac{6930}{9000}, \frac{7000}{9000}$ or</td><td>$.009, .770, .777\frac{7}{9}$ or</td></tr>
<tr><td>$.9\% < .77 < \frac{7}{9}$</td><td>$.9\% < .77 < \frac{7}{9}$</td></tr>
</table>

Write these numbers in order from smallest to largest.
Write them all as fractions or decimals first.

$\frac{1}{10}$, .09, 2%   100%, .33$\frac{1}{3}$, 1$\frac{1}{2}$ .33, 3.3%, $\frac{3}{10}$

1. $\frac{1}{10} =$ _____   5. 100% = _____   9. .33 = _____

2. .09 = _____   6. .33$\frac{1}{3}$ = _____   10. 3.3% = _____

3. 2% = _____   7. 1$\frac{1}{2}$ = _____   11. $\frac{3}{10}$ = _____

4. _____, _____, _____   8. _____, _____, _____   12. _____, _____, _____

For extra practice see page 137.

Objective/Compare fractions, decimals, and percents.

Posttest/Unit 2

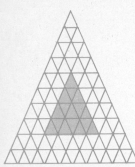

Find answers 4–21 by changing the percent, decimal, or fraction to the other forms.

	Fraction	Decimal	Percent

1. What percent of the triangle is green?

_____

2. What percent of the triangle is white?

_____

3. What percent of the triangle has been divided into smaller triangles?

_____

4. _____
5. _____   95%

6. _____   1.00   7. _____
   $\frac{1}{8}$ 8. _____   9. _____

10. _____
11. _____   280%

12. _____   .006   13. _____
   $\frac{1}{500}$ 14. _____   15. _____

16. _____
17. _____   1.6%

18. _____ $.16\frac{2}{3}$ 19. _____
   $\frac{1}{2}$ 20. _____   21. _____

Write in order from the largest to the smallest.

22. .83, $\frac{5}{6}$,   8.4%

23. .11%,   .5, $\frac{1}{5}$

24. $\frac{1}{2}$,   .55%,   .55

_____, _____, _____   _____, _____, _____   _____, _____, _____

25. $\frac{1}{3}$,   33%,   .35

26. 63%, $\frac{6}{10}$,   6.3

27. 4.2%, $4\frac{1}{2}$,   4.55

_____, _____, _____   _____, _____, _____   _____, _____, _____

28. The air we breathe is one-fifth oxygen. Write that as a percent.   _____

29. Nitrogen is .78 of the air. Write that as a percent.   _____

30. .93% of air is argon. Write that as a decimal.   _____

28

KEY/Lesson 10   3
Lesson 11   1, 2
Lesson 13   5, 11, 17, 30
Lesson 14   7, 13, 19, 29
Lesson 15   4, 10, 16
Lesson 16   9, 15, 21, 28
Lesson 17   6, 8, 12, 14, 18, 20, 22–27

Pretest/Unit 3
Solving percent problems

Solve these percent problems.

1. 50% of 880 is what? _____

2. 80% of what is 24? _____

3. 6 is what percent of 72? _____

4. What is 75% of 1000? _____

5. 15% of what is 900? _____

6. .3% of what is 27? _____

7. $\frac{1}{2}$ is what percent of $\frac{3}{4}$? _____

8. 275% of what is 550? _____

9. 20% of .4 is what? _____

10. 57 is what percent of 19? _____

Decide what answer fits in the blank. Write it on the answer line below.

"Mike and I plan to buy a freezer so we can buy larger amounts of meat on sale," said Carol.

11. "There's a sale on freezers at Lake's. They're 25% off the regular price. You'll save $_____ on a $400 freezer," said Alice.

_____

12. "You would pay $_____ for the freezer."

_____

13. "Yes, then I have to include $6\frac{1}{2}$% sales tax on the sale price. That's $_____."

_____

14. "The delivery charge is $9.00 or _____% of the sale price."

_____

15. "Then the total cost of the freezer is $_____," said Alice.

_____

Lesson 18
Recognizing percent problems

All percents are based on 100.
All percent problems are made up of four things:
the **whole**, the **part**, the **percent**, and **100**.
The percent always has a **%**.
The whole is always after the word **of**.
The word **what** tells whether the whole, the part, or the percent is missing.

Use a grid to place the four parts of a percent problem.
The **100** is always in the lower right corner.
The **percent** is always on top of the 100.
The **whole** is always in the lower left corner.
The **part** is always on top of the whole.

part	percent
whole	100

A. 50% of what is 15?

part 15	percent 50
whole ?	100

The percent is 50 because
it has a %.
The whole is missing
because the word after
of is **what**.
The part is 15.

B. 15 is what percent of 30?

part 15	percent ?
whole 30	100

The percent is missing
because the problem
says **what** percent.
The whole is 30 because
it follows the word **of**.
The part is 15.

C. What is 50% of 30?

part ?	percent 50
whole 30	100

The percent is 50 because
it has a %.
The whole is 30 because
it follows the word **of**.
The part is missing.

Place the whole, the part, and the percent in the grid for each of these problems. Place a ? for the missing piece of information.

1. What percent of 50 is 30?

part	percent
whole	100

2. 16 is 60% of what?

part	percent
whole	100

3. 10 is 30% of what?

part	percent
whole	100

4. 4 is what percent of 20?

part	percent
whole	100

5. 25% of 80 is what?

part	percent
whole	100

6. 22 is 1% of what?

part	percent
whole	100

7. What is 9% of 81?

part	percent
whole	100

8. What percent of 90 is 45?

part	percent
whole	100

9. 1% of what is 2?

part	percent
whole	100

10. What is 45% of 5?

part	percent
whole	100

Objective/Recognize percent problems.

Lesson 19
Solving for the whole

Rules:

1. Place the known information in the grid.
2. Multiply the diagonals (cross-products).
3. Divide the answer by the number that is left.

A. 65% of what is 130?

1.

part	percent
130	**65**
whole	
?	**100**

2. $130 \times 100 = 13{,}000$

3.
$$
\begin{array}{r}
200 \\
65\overline{)13{,}000} \\
\underline{13\ 0} \\
00
\end{array}
$$

The answer is 200.

65% of 200 is 130.

B. $33\frac{1}{3}$% of what is 45?

1.

part	percent
45	**33¹/₃**
whole	
?	**100**

2. $45 \times 100 = 4500$

3. $4500 \div 33\frac{1}{3} =$

$$\frac{4500}{1} \div \frac{100}{3} =$$

$$\frac{\overset{45}{\cancel{4500}}}{1} \times \frac{3}{\underset{1}{\cancel{100}}} = 135$$

The answer is 135.

$33\frac{1}{3}$% of 135 is 45.

Draw a grid for each of these problems and then solve.

1. 1% of what is 2? _____

2. $87\frac{1}{2}$% of what is 490? _____

3. 77 is 15% of what? _____

4. 20 is 7% of what? _____

5. $33\frac{1}{3}$% of what is 6? _____

6. 150% of what is 6? _____

7. $\frac{1}{2}$% of what is 88? _____

8. 440 is 55% of what? _____

9. .3% of what is 21? _____

10. 2.3% of what is .92? _____

Circle the letter of the correct answer to each problem. Study the example first.

Tommaso spent 20% of his annual income on a car. If the car was $3500, how much does he earn?

a. $17,500.00   b. $17.50   c. $3500.00   d. $1750.00

Read the problem. Look for the whole, the part, and the percent.
   20% is the percent. $3500 is the part.
Draw a grid. Put the known information in the correct places.
Decide how to solve the problem.
   Multiply $3500 by 100.
   Divide by 20.
Choose the best answer by estimating and ruling out obviously wrong answers.
   His income has to be more than the price of the car, so choose **a.**
Check by working the problem.
   $3500 × 100 = $350,000
   $350,000 ÷ 20 = $17,500

part	percent
3500	**20**
whole	
?	**100**

11. Luis paid $22.00 tax on the furniture he bought. If the sales tax is 4%, what was the cost of the furniture?

   a. $550   b. $55.00   c. $181.18   d. $1818.18

12. The Moys paid $139.00 real estate tax on their home. If the tax is $\frac{1}{4}$% of the value of their home, what is the home worth?

   a. $34,750.00   b. $3475.00   c. $5560.00   d. $55,600.00

13. Neil received a $3.40 tip. It was 10% of the cost of the meal. What was the cost of the meal?

   a. $340   b. $34.00   c. $29.41   d. $294.10

14. In order to buy a townhome, the Pewrlas had to make an $8000 down payment. This was 25% of the purchase price. What was the cost of the townhome?

   a. $32,000.00   b. $31,250.00   c. $3,200.00   d. $3,125.00

15. For every appliance Aretha sells, she gets a 20% commission. If she earned $320.00 last month, how many dollars' worth of appliances did she sell?

   a. $6400   b. $160.00   c. $1600   d. $3125

For extra practice see page 138.

Objective/Solve for the whole.

0   12   15

Life skill
Percents and sale prices

SALE 33⅓% OFF

heavy-duty
staple gun
$14.66

5-foot
wooden ladder
$14.88

air filter
$1.86

fireplace
grate
$10.60

4-inch paintbrush
$4.18

14-inch
push
broom
$1.98

snow brush and scraper
$1.24

50-foot vinyl hose
$8.30

8-inch pruner
$3.98

Solve these problems using the information from the ad. The solutions for #1 and #2 are given.

1. The staple gun is on sale for ___$14.66___.
   The answer is given in the ad.

2. The original price was ___$21.99___.

   "33⅓% off" means that the sale price (the part) is 66⅔% of the original price (the whole).

   $66\frac{2}{3}\% = \frac{2}{3}$

   The whole = $14.66 ÷ $\frac{2}{3}$.
   = $21.99, the original price.

3. The snow brush and scraper is on sale for _____.

4. The original price was _____.

5. The fireplace grate is on sale for _____.

6. The original price was _____.

7. The pruner is on sale for _____.

8. The original price was _____.

9. The ladder is on sale for _____.

10. The original price was _____.

11. The paintbrush is on sale for _____.

12. The original price was _____.

Objective/Solve for the whole.

Lesson 20
Solving for the part

Rules:
1. Place the known information in the grid.
2. Multiply the diagonals (cross-products).
3. Divide the answer by the number that is left.

A. **What is $8\frac{1}{3}\%$ of 240?**

1.

part	percent
?	**8¹/₃**
whole	
240	**100**

2. $8\frac{1}{3} \times 240 =$

$$\frac{25}{\overset{}{3}_{1}} \times \frac{\overset{80}{240}}{1} = 2000$$

3.
$$\begin{array}{r} 20 \\ 100\overline{)2000} \\ \underline{200} \\ 0 \end{array}$$

The answer is 20.

20 is $8\frac{1}{3}\%$ of 240.

B. **.5% of 300 is what?**

1.

part	percent
?	**.5**
whole	
300	**100**

2.
$$\begin{array}{r} 300 \\ \times\ .5 \\ \hline 150.0 \end{array}$$

3.
$$\begin{array}{r} 1.5 \\ 100\overline{)150.0} \\ \underline{100} \\ 50\ 0 \\ \underline{50\ 0} \end{array}$$

The answer is 1.5.

.5% of 300 is 1.5.

Draw a grid for each of these problems and then solve.

1. What is 5% of 275? _____

2. What is $166\frac{2}{3}\%$ of 300? _____

3. What is 58% of 440? _____

4. What is $83\frac{1}{3}\%$ of 5400? _____

5. What is $\frac{1}{4}\%$ of 440? _____

6. 345% of 12 is what? _____

7. 77.05% of 958 is what? _____

8. 400% of 3 is what? _____

9. 4% of 56 is what? _____

10. 100% of 891 is what? _____

Objective/Solve for the part.

Fill in the space under the letter of the correct answer to each problem. Study the example first.

Leon Vega earns $530 every pay period. 15% of his salary is withheld for state and federal income tax. How much is withheld?

a. $35.33   b. $79.50   c. $7.95   d. $17.95

a	b	c	d
‖	▮	‖	‖

Read the problem. Look for the whole, the part, and the percent.
        $530 is the whole. 15% is the percent.
Draw a grid. Put the known information in the correct places.
Decide how to solve the problem.
        Multiply 15 by $530.
        Divide by 100.

part	percent
?	15
whole	
530	100

Choose the best answer by estimating and ruling out obviously wrong answers.
        10% of $500 is $50, so **a, c,** and **d** would be too small.
Check by working the problem.

```
  $530              $   79.50
 × 15          100)$7950.00
 2650              700
  530              950
$7950              900
                   500
                   500
                     0
```

11. 32% of the vote has been counted. If 775 people voted, how many votes have been counted so far?

    a. 2214   b. 270   c. 150   d. 248

a	b	c	d
‖	‖	‖	‖

12. $62\frac{1}{2}$% of the people polled did not agree with the Senate's vote. If 8000 people were polled, how many did not agree?

    a. 50   b. 5000   c. 500   d. 5

a	b	c	d
‖	‖	‖	‖

13. Shams got a 20% rebate on the shaver he bought for $32.50. How much money did he get back?

    a. $6.50   b. $.65   c. $6.25   d. $6.00

a	b	c	d
‖	‖	‖	‖

14. Sue Ellen bought a desk for $44.00. After she refinished it, she sold it at 150% of its original price. What did she sell it for?

    a. $66.00   b. $22.00   c. $48.00   d. $77.50

a	b	c	d
‖	‖	‖	‖

15. 38% of the families in a neighborhood are against having a park nearby. If there are 200 families in the area, how many are against the park?

    a. 86   b. 95   c. 43   d. 76

a	b	c	d
‖	‖	‖	‖

For extra practice see page 139.

0   12   15

Objective/Solve for the part.

Life skill
Shopping at a sale

J.D. is shopping for a stereo. His friend is helping him figure out how much it will cost. Help them out by finding answers for the blanks in these problems.

1. "I just found out that the $240 stereo set I wanted is on sale for 25% off," shouted J.D. "That works out to $_____ off."

   _____

2. "That means you only have to pay $_____ for the whole set," said Al.

   _____

3. "Well, I need to get some wires too," said J.D. "They are 20% off the regular price of $1.85 each. So I save $_____ on each one."

   _____

4. "OK, so each one costs $_____. How many do you need?" said Al.

   _____

5. "Six," said J.D. "That's a total of $_____."

   _____

6. Al then asked, "Are you going to get any of those $5.00 tapes? At 30% off, you'll save $_____ on each one of them."

   _____

7. "Let's see, that means each one would cost $_____," J.D. said.

   _____

8. Al added, "You could pick up five tapes for $_____."

   _____

9. "I should figure up my whole bill before I go," J.D. said. "That works out to $_____ before the sales tax."

   _____

Lesson 21
Solving for the percent

Rules:
1. Place the known information in the grid.
2. Multiply the diagonals (cross-products).
3. Divide the answer by the number that is left.

A. $\frac{3}{4}$ **is what percent of** $\frac{1}{2}$**?**

1.
part	percent
³/₄	?
whole	
¹/₂	**100**

2. $\frac{3}{4} \times 100 =$

   $\frac{3}{4} \times \frac{\overset{25}{\cancel{100}}}{1} = 75$

3. $75 \div \frac{1}{2} =$

   $\frac{75}{1} \times \frac{2}{1} = 150$

The answer is 150%.

$\frac{3}{4}$ is 150% of $\frac{1}{2}$.

B. **What percent of 125 is 62.5?**

1.
part	percent
62.5	?
whole	
125	**100**

2. $62.5 \times 100 = 6250$

3. $$125\overline{)6250}$$ $= 50$
   $$\underline{625}$$
   $$0$$

The answer is 50%.

50% of 125 is 62.5.

Draw a grid for each of these problems and then solve.

1. 25 is what percent of 75? _____

2. What percent of 500 is 50? _____

3. 66 is what percent of 132? _____

4. 4 is what percent of 8? _____

5. .5 is what percent of 1.5? _____

6. 24 is what percent of 8? _____

7. $\frac{1}{3}$ is what percent of $\frac{5}{6}$? _____

8. $78\frac{1}{2}$ is what percent of 628? _____

9. .39 is what percent of 1.17? _____

10. What percent of .25 is .05? _____

Objective/Solve for the percent.

Fill in the space under the letter of the correct answer to each problem. Study the example first.

At the day care center, 58 of the 145 children were under three years old. What percent of the children were under three?

a. 2.5%   b. 4%   c. 25%   d. 40%

a	b	c	d
‖	‖	‖	▌

part	percent
58	**?**
whole	
145	**100**

Read the problem. Look for the whole, the part, and the percent.
    145 is the whole. 58 is the part.
Draw a grid. Put the known information in the correct places.
Decide how to solve the problem.
    Multiply 100 by 58.
    Divide by 145.
Choose the best answer by estimating and ruling out obviously wrong answers.
    60 is a little less than half of 140, so choose **d**.
Check by working the problem.

$$100 \times 58 = 5800$$

$$145\overline{)5800}$$
$$\underline{580}$$
$$0$$

with quotient 40

The answer is 40%.

11. Out of the 51 questions on the test, Victor got 34 right. What percent of the total is that?

a. 1.5%   b. $33\frac{1}{3}$%   c. 15%   d. $66\frac{2}{3}$%

a	b	c	d
‖	‖	‖	‖

12. Julio pays $7.20 a month in union dues. He earns $900.00 a month. What percent of his total pay is his union dues?

a. 8%   b. .8%   c. 80%   d. 12.5%

a	b	c	d
‖	‖	‖	‖

13. The Parks left a tip of $1.80 for a $15.00 meal. What was the percent tip they left the waitress?

a. 1.2%   b. 12%   c. $8\frac{1}{3}$%   d. 83%

a	b	c	d
‖	‖	‖	‖

14. The Jeffersons paid $116.00 in real estate taxes on their $29,000 condominium. What is their tax percentage rate?

a. 25%   b. 400%   c. .4%   d. 40%

a	b	c	d
‖	‖	‖	‖

15. Josh and Nina can buy a good used dining room set for $120.00 A similar new one would cost $360.00. The used furniture price is what percent of the price of the new furniture?

a. $33\frac{1}{3}$%   b. $\frac{3}{10}$%   c. $\frac{1}{3}$%   d. 30%

a	b	c	d
‖	‖	‖	‖

For extra practice see page 140.

0   12   15

Objective/Solve for the percent.

Life skill
Percents and budgeting

Takeo and Vicki Ogata were trying to find out where all their money goes. They decided to figure out what percent of their income they spend on each budget item. Help them by finding answers for the blanks in these problems.

1. "My net salary is $492 a month and yours is $628 a month," said Vicki. "Our total take-home pay is $_____ a month."

   _____

2. "We spend $280.00 a month on rent. That's _____ percent of our total income," said Takeo.

   _____

3. "Don't forget our car payment. It's $140.00 a month," said Vicki. "That is _____ percent of our total income."

   _____

4. "We spend $112 for gasoline and parking each month," said Takeo. "That works out to be _____ percent of our income."

   _____

5. Vicki added, "$224.00 a month goes for food. So that is _____ percent of our income."

   _____

6. "I think I'd better sign up for that medical insurance policy at work. It's $5.60 a month and only _____ percent of our income. It might save us money later," said Takeo.

   _____

7. "If we saved $100.00 a month, that would be only _____ percent of our income," said Vicki. "And at the end of a year we'll have money for new furniture."

   _____

8. "That leaves us with $_____ for things like clothes, movies, and bowling," said Takeo.

   _____

Lesson 22
Deciding how to solve a percent problem

Here is how to solve the three kinds of percent problems.

Rules:
1. Place the known information in the grid.
2. Multiply the diagonals (cross-products).
3. Divide the answer by the number that is left.

A. Solving for the whole
83% of what is 332?

1.

part	percent
332	**83**
whole	
?	**100**

2. $332 \times 100 = 33{,}200$

3.
$$\begin{array}{r} 400 \\ 83\overline{)33{,}200} \\ 33\ 2 \\ \hline 00 \\ 00 \end{array}$$

The answer is 400.

B. Solving for the part
What is $16\frac{2}{3}\%$ of 1500?

1.

part	percent
?	**16²/₃**
whole	
1500	**100**

2. $1500 \times 16\frac{2}{3} =$

$$\frac{\overset{500}{\cancel{1500}}}{1} \times \frac{50}{\underset{1}{\cancel{3}}} = 25{,}000$$

3.
$$\begin{array}{r} 250 \\ 100\overline{)25{,}000} \\ 20\ 0 \\ \hline 5\ 00 \\ 5\ 00 \\ \hline 0 \end{array}$$

The answer is 250.

C. Solving for the percent
$\frac{4}{5}$ is what percent of $\frac{1}{5}$?

1.

part	percent
⁴/₅	**?**
whole	
¹/₅	**100**

2. $\frac{4}{5} \times 100 =$

$$\frac{4}{\underset{1}{\cancel{5}}} \times \frac{\overset{20}{\cancel{100}}}{1} = 80$$

3. $80 \div \frac{1}{5} =$

$$\frac{80}{1} \times \frac{5}{1} = 400$$

The answer is 400%.

Draw a grid for each of these problems and then solve.

1. 75% of what is 225? _____

2. 6 is what percent of 18? _____

3. What is 10% of 1243? _____

4. 177 is 60% of what? _____

5. .5 is what percent of 2? _____

6. What is 200% of 445? _____

7. $\frac{1}{2}$% of what is 9? _____

8. 9 is what percent of 81? _____

9. What is $7\frac{1}{4}$% of 4900? _____

10. 100% of what is 2793? _____

Objective/Solve percent problems.

Find the answers.

11. What percent of $\frac{1}{2}$ is $\frac{1}{10}$? _____

12. What is 66% of 80? _____

13. 90% of what is 270? _____

14. What percent of 70 is .7? _____

15. What is .05% of 250? _____

16. 8% of what is 48? _____

17. 12 is .5% of what? _____

18. What percent is 6.3 of 126? _____

19. What is $33\frac{1}{3}$% of 3300? _____

20. $8\frac{1}{3}$% of what is 12? _____

21. 36 is what percent of 9? _____

22. What is 25% of 1600? _____

Solve these problems.

23. 4800 students enrolled in a community college are over the age of 25. That is 60% of the total enrollment. What is the total enrollment?

_____

24. 80% of the people who took a basic skills review class went on to college. If there were 90 people in the class, how many went on?

_____

25. 9 people in the basic skills course had to change shifts at their jobs. What percent of the class had to change shifts?

_____

26. 66% of the class said that they came back to school in order to find a job or to get a promotion. How many came back to school for those reasons?

_____

27. 81 people said they would tell their friends about the program. That is what percent of the members of the class?

_____

28. 54 students finished the course in eight weeks. What percent was that?

_____

For extra practice see pages 141, 142, 143 and 144.

0   22   28

Objective/Solve percent problems.

Life skill
Percents in business

Budgeting overhead expenses

The Rodriguez family manages a small neighborhood grocery. Their total budget for this grocery is $3500 a month. What percent of the budget is spent on the following overhead expenses?

1. $420.00 for renting space _____ %

2. $144.00 for utilities and maintenance _____ %

3. $120.00 for advertising _____ %

4. $12.00 for licenses _____ %

Earning commission

The four salespeople at Nick's Used Car Lot get a 14% commission on the price of every car they sell. Their earnings for two weeks are given below. If this is what they earned on commission, how many dollars worth of cars did each sell?

5. Toni Lugotti — $447.30 _____

6. Frank Mason — $351.40 _____

7. Juanita Alvarez — $402.22 _____

8. Susan Josephson — $527.10 _____

Finding sales tax

Martha works in a restaurant. She needs to add $5\frac{1}{2}$% sales tax to the price of each dinner. Here is a list of her bills for Saturday. Find the sales tax on each one.

9. $10.00 _____

10. $32.00 _____

11. $26.00 _____

12. $158.00 _____

Definitions of overhead, commission, and sales tax are in the word list on page 135.

Objective/Understand overhead, commission, and sales tax.

Posttest/Unit 3

Find the percent, the whole, or the part.

1. 341 is what percent of 62? _____

2. 57% of 1000 is what? _____

3. 8% of what is 144? _____

4. 42 is what percent of 126? _____

5. 90% of 476 is what? _____

6. 16% of what is 466? _____

7. $\frac{1}{2}$ is what percent of $\frac{3}{4}$? _____

8. .75% of .5 is what? _____

9. 3.5% of what is 16.94? _____

10. 42.25 is what percent of 380.25? _____

Wayne and Judy Whitebird plan to buy a washer and dryer with their tax refund. Help them figure the cost by finding answers for the blanks.

11. "Johnson's Department Store has a washer-dryer pair on sale at 80% of its regular price. If it's $400.00 now, it must have cost $_____ originally," said Wayne.

_____

12. "Don't forget, they charge a delivery and installation fee that is 9.5% of the sale price," said Judy. "That's an extra $_____."

_____

13. "We also have to add $6\frac{1}{2}$% sales tax to the sale price," Wayne said. "That's $_____."

_____

14. "We'll get a trade-in worth 3.5% of the sale price on our old machines. That's $_____ off."

_____

15. "The total price for the washer and dryer is $_____," said Judy.

_____

16. "The sale price is $400.00. That's _____% of the final total," said Wayne.

_____

Pretest/Unit 4
Using percents

Find the amount of interest on the following.

1. a loan of $850 at 18% a year for one year and four months _____

2. a $1000 savings certificate at 6% a year for six months _____

Find answers for the blanks in these problems.

3. "The newspaper says there is a sale on carpeting at Franklin Furniture. Rugs selling for $660 are now on sale for $440. That is a _____% discount," said Mrs. Chen to her husband. _____

4. "It says that we could put 20% down and pay $35.91 a month for a year," said Mr. Chen. "That's a down payment of $_____." _____

5. "Twelve monthly payments would add up to $_____," said Mrs. Chen. _____

6. "That makes the total cost of the rug $_____," Mr. Chen figured. _____

7. "That is a _____% increase over the sale price of the rug," said Mrs. Chen. _____

8. "Well," said Mr. Chen, "we could take out a loan from the bank for $450 at 12% interest for a year. That would be $_____ in interest." _____

9. "With the loan from the bank, we would pay a total of $_____ for the rug," said Mrs. Chen. _____

10. "We would save $_____ by using the bank instead of the installment plan. I think that is much wiser," said Mr. Chen. _____

Lesson 23
Simple interest

Interest is the cost of borrowing money.
Principal is the amount of money being borrowed.
Rate is the percent of the principal being paid per year as interest.
Time is the length of the loan expressed in years.

Simple interest problems are like percent problems except interest problems always include time.

$$\text{part} \quad = \text{whole} \times \text{percent}$$

$$\text{interest} = \text{principal} \times \text{rate} \times \text{time}$$

Interest is the part, rate is the percent (per year), and principal is the whole.

To solve interest problems, the percent (rate) must be changed to a fraction or a decimal. Study these examples.

A.
What is the interest on $4692.00 at 11% for 1 year?

1. $11\% = .11. = .11$

2. $\text{interest} = \text{principal} \times \text{rate} \times \text{time}$

$$= \frac{\$4692}{1} \times \frac{.11}{\text{yr.}} \times \frac{1 \text{ yr.}}{1}$$

$$= \$516.12$$

B.
What is the interest on $890.00 at 7.5% for 1 year?

1. $7.5\% = .07.5 = .075$

2. $\text{interest} = \text{principal} \times \text{rate} \times \text{time}$

$$= \frac{\$890.00}{1} \times \frac{.075}{\text{yr.}} \times \frac{1 \text{ yr.}}{1}$$

$$= \$66.75$$

C.
What is the interest on $840 at $5\frac{1}{4}$% for 1 year?

1. $5\frac{1}{4}\% = \frac{21}{4} \times \frac{1}{100} = \frac{21}{400}$

2. $\text{interest} = \frac{\$840}{1} \times \frac{\frac{21}{400}}{\text{yr.}} \times \frac{1 \text{ yr.}}{1}$

$$= \frac{\overset{21}{\cancel{\$840}}}{1} \times \frac{21}{\underset{10}{\cancel{400}}} \times 1$$

$$= \$44.10$$

Solve the following interest problems.
What is the interest on

1. $200.00 at 9.75% for 1 year?

   _____

2. $362.00 at 5% for 1 year?

   _____

3. $7040.00 at $4\frac{3}{4}$% for 1 year?

   _____

4. $184.00 at $6\frac{1}{4}$% for 1 year?

   _____

5. $2150 at 4.5% for 1 year?

   _____

6. $169.00 at 12% for 1 year?

   _____

Find the answers for the blanks in these problems.

7. "T.R., with your $1800 and my $2325 we have $54\frac{3}{4}$% of what we need to open our own body shop. All we need is a small business loan for the other $45\frac{1}{4}$%," said Fred.
   "That means we have to borrow $_____," said T.R.

   _____

8. "Look," said Fred, "at $11\frac{3}{4}$% we only pay $_____ in interest per year."

   _____

9. "Don't forget that I'm still paying $118 a month on my truck," cut in T.R. "That's 32% of my monthly pay. You know I make $_____ a month."

   _____

10. "If we start working together, I promise your salary will go up 65% at least. That's $_____ a month," said Fred.

    _____

Objective/Find simple interest.

0   8   10

Lesson 24
Simple interest for less than or more than one year

In simple interest problems, time is always given in terms of a year.

To find interest for **less than one year,** write the time in the problem as a fraction of a year. One month can be written as $\frac{1}{12}$ year. 8 months can be written

$$\frac{8}{12} \text{ year} = \frac{2}{3} \text{ year.}$$

A.
What is the interest on $3900 at 3% for 6 months?

time: 6 months $= \frac{6}{12}$ yr. $= \frac{1}{2}$ yr.

rate: $\dfrac{3\%}{\text{yr.}} = \dfrac{\frac{3}{1} \times \frac{1}{100}}{\text{yr.}} = \dfrac{\frac{3}{100}}{\text{yr.}}$

principal $\times$ rate $\times$ time $=$ interest

$\dfrac{\$3900}{1} \times \dfrac{3}{100} \times \dfrac{1}{2} = \dfrac{\$117}{2} = \$58.50$

B.
What is the interest for $600 at $7\frac{1}{2}$% for 3 months?

time: 3 months $= \frac{3}{12}$ yr. $= \frac{1}{4}$ yr.

rate: $\dfrac{7\frac{1}{2}\%}{\text{yr.}} = \dfrac{\frac{15}{2} \times \frac{1}{100}}{\text{yr.}} = \dfrac{\frac{3}{40}}{\text{yr.}}$

principal $\times$ rate $\times$ time $=$ interest

$\dfrac{\$600}{1} \times \dfrac{3}{40} \times \dfrac{1}{4} = \dfrac{\$45}{4} = \$11.25$

To find interest for **more than one year,** write whole years as whole numbers. If the time is more than one year and part of another, write the mixed number as an improper fraction or decimal.

C.
What is the interest on $542 at 3% for 2 years?

time: 2 years

rate: $\dfrac{3\%}{\text{yr.}} = \dfrac{.03}{\text{yr.}}$

principal $\times$ rate $\times$ time $=$ interest

$\$542 \times .03 \times 2 = \$32.52$

D.
What is the interest on $7500 at $5\frac{1}{2}$% for 2 years 6 months?

time: 2 years 6 months $= 2\frac{1}{2}$ yr. $= \frac{5}{2}$ yr.

rate: $\dfrac{5\frac{1}{2}\%}{\text{yr.}} = \dfrac{\frac{11}{2} \times \frac{1}{100}}{\text{yr.}} = \dfrac{\frac{11}{200}}{\text{yr.}}$

principal $\times$ rate $\times$ time $=$ interest

$\dfrac{\$7500}{1} \times \dfrac{11}{200} \times \dfrac{5}{2} = \$1031.25$

Objective/Find simple interest for more or less than one year.

Solve. What is the interest on

1. $2000.00 at 5% for 3 months?

_____

2. $625.00 at 6.8% for 6 months?

_____

3. $1025.00 at 4% for 9 months?

_____

4. $9000.00 at 9.75% for 4 months?

_____

5. $600.00 at $5\frac{1}{2}$% for 9 months?

_____

6. $2800.00 at $10\frac{3}{4}$% for 6 months?

_____

7. $1760.00 at $4\frac{3}{4}$% for 3 years?

_____

8. $150.00 at $7\frac{1}{2}$% for 2 years?

_____

9. $1300.00 at 5% for 6 years?

_____

10. $3600.00 at 6.5% for 1 year and 4 months?

_____

11. $1570.00 at 12% for 2 years and 8 months?

_____

12. $2620.00 at $15\frac{1}{2}$% for 3 years?

_____

Objective/Find simple interest for more or less than one year.

51

Find the interest on the following.

13. $246.00 in a savings account for 2 years at 5%

_____

16. a $1000.00 savings certificate at 6.25% for 3 months

_____

14. a car loan of $3472.00 at 14% for 18 months

_____

17. $755 in a $5\frac{1}{2}$% savings account for 4 years

_____

15. $982.00 in a 3-month savings certificate at 6%

_____

18. a furniture loan of $592.80 at $12\frac{1}{3}$% for $1\frac{1}{2}$ years

_____

Find interest on the following. Blacken the space under the letter of the correct answer to each problem.

19. a 4.5% home improvement loan for $7562.00 for three years

    a. $10.21   **c.** $1020.87
    b. $102.09   **d.** $340.29

    a   b   c   d
   || || || ||

20. a $1245 education loan at 7% for 4 years

    a. $348.60   **c.** $87.15
    b. $3486.00   **d.** $49.80

    a   b   c   d
   || || || ||

21. a car loan of $2610.00 at 6.5% for 2 years and 8 months

    a. $45.24   **c.** $169.65
    b. $452.40   **d.** $339.30

    a   b   c   d
   || || || ||

22. a $9\frac{3}{4}$% medical loan for $3720 for 5 years and 4 months

    a. $192.40   **c.** $360.75
    b. $1934.40   **d.** $3607.50

    a   b   c   d
   || || || ||

To learn how to find compound interest by using a calculator see page 145.

0   18   22

Objective/Find simple interest for more or less than one year.

Lesson 25

Installment plan buying

Installment plan buying means paying a certain percent of the purchase price as a **down payment** and agreeing to pay the rest in small amounts each month. The monthly amounts include an interest payment. This type of interest is called a **finance charge.**

Connie bought a furniture set on sale for $350.00. She put 10% down and paid $30.00 a month for a year. What total amount did she pay?

Down payment = $350 × .10 = $35.00
$30 a month for 12 months   = $360.00
Total cost of furniture $395.00

Solve.

1. Yao wants to buy a color TV for $399.00. The store says he can put 15% down and pay $33.30 a month for 12 months. What is the down payment?   _____

2. What are the total monthly payments?   _____

3. What is the total cost of the TV?   _____

4. If Yao took out a loan for $399.00 at 9%, how much would the loan cost for one year?   _____

5. What is the difference in cost between the installment plan and the loan?   _____

        Objective/Solve installment plan problems.

6. The Silvas want to buy a boat that costs $475.00. They have to put 25% down and pay $35 a month for a year. What is the down payment?

_____

7. What are the total monthly payments?

_____

8. What is the total cost of the boat when they pay on the installment plan?

_____

9. If the Silvas took out a loan of $475.00 at 10%, what would the cost of the loan be?

_____

10. What is the difference in cost between the installment plan and the loan?

_____

11. The Lees put 8% down on the $188.00 worth of camping gear they bought. They are paying $16.50 a month for a year. What was the down payment?

_____

12. What are their total monthly payments?

_____

13. What is the total cost of the camping gear?

_____

14. If they had taken out a loan of $190.00 at 7.5%, what would the loan have cost?

_____

15. What is the difference in cost between the installment plan and the loan?

_____

For extra practice see pages 146 and 147.

0   12   15

Objective/Solve installment plan problems.

Lesson 26
Percent of increase or decrease

Finding the **percent of increase** takes two steps.
1. Subtract the original amount from the new amount.
2. Divide the difference by the original amount.

$$\frac{\text{new amount } - \text{ original amount}}{\text{original amount}} = \text{percent of increase}$$

The Mahoneys wanted to buy a car last year for $6650.00. This year the same model is priced at $7315.00 What is the percent of increase?

new amount = $7315.00   original price = $6650.00

$$\frac{\$7315 - \$6650}{\$6650} = 10\% \quad \text{(percent of increase)}$$

Solve.

1. The price of pork changed from $1.68 a pound to $1.89 a pound. Did the price increase or decrease? By what percent did the price increase or decrease?   _____

    _____

2. The weekly wages of a chef rose from $224 to $264 in three years. What was the percent of increase?   _____

3. Matt and Dot Washington bought a town house for $50,000 five years ago. They just sold it for $64,000. What was the percent of increase in the value of their home?   _____

Objective/Find the percent of increase.

Finding the **percent of decrease** takes two steps.
1. Subtract the new amount from the original amount.
2. Divide the difference by the original amount.

$$\frac{\text{original amount} - \text{new amount}}{\text{original amount}} = \text{percent of decrease}$$

Manuel Chavez bought a new car 2 years ago for $5642. He sold it last week for $3103.10. What was the percent of decrease in the value of his car?

original price = $5642   **new amount** = $3103.10

$$\frac{\$5642 - \$3103.10}{\$5642} = 45\% \quad \textbf{(percent of decrease)}$$

Solve.

4. Henry bought a turntable on sale for $100.00. It originally sold for $175.00. What was the percent of decrease?   _____

5. The price of a fabric dropped from $5.50 per yard to $4.30 per yard during a sale. What was the percent of decrease?   _____

6. Portable radios decreased in price from $25.00 to $15.00 in the past five years. What is the percent of decrease?   _____

7. Last year in Redvale, an average of 11,400 people rode the city buses each weekday. This year the average is 15,200. What is the percent of increase?

_____

8. The Godziks' taxes were raised from $50.00 to $65.00 a year. What is the percent of increase?

_____

9. Casey bought an oven last year for $300.00. This year it was selling for $250.00. What was the percent of decrease in the selling price?

_____

10. Darla's father bought a gold watch fifty years ago for $25.00. The watch is now worth $600.00. What is the percent of increase in the value of the watch?

_____

11. Werner bought a cycle on sale for $2502.50. It originally cost $2750. What was the percent of decrease?

_____

12. When the minimum wage rose from $2.90 to $3.10 an hour, what was the percent of increase? (Round to the nearest whole percent.)

_____

For extra practice see page 148.

Objective/Find the percent of increase or decrease.

0   10   12

Posttest/Unit 4

Find the amount of interest on the following.

1. an insurance policy loan for $200 at 7% for 9 months _____

2. a $2342 savings account at 4.5% for 6 years and 4 months _____

Find answers for the blanks in these problems.

3. "Ray, I've decided to get Lisa a ring. I talked to Oscar at Star Jewelers. He says he will sell a $500 ring for $275. That's a _____% decrease," said Derrick. _____

4. "I thought I'd buy it on the installment plan at 8% down and a year to pay. Then I'd only have to pay $_____ on it now and $24 a month for a year," said Derrick. _____

5. "Derrick, that makes a total of $_____ that you are going to pay for the ring," Ray said. _____

6. "Hey, that's a _____% increase over the original price of $275," said Derrick. _____

7. "If you went to the Navy Credit Union," said Ray, "you could borrow $275 at 11% interest for a year, and the interest would be only $_____." _____

8. "That would make my total cost $_____," said Derrick. _____

9. "That's a difference of $_____ between Star's installment plan and the credit union's loan," said Ray. _____

10. "And if I put that difference in a savings account at 6% for one year, I'll earn $_____," Derrick said. _____

Percents

Change the percent, decimal, or fraction to the other forms.

Percent	Decimal	Fraction
15%	1. _____	2. _____
3. _____	.50	4. _____
5. _____	6. _____	$\frac{1}{4}$
$33\frac{1}{3}\%$	7. _____	8. _____
9. _____	$.83\frac{1}{3}$	10. _____
115%	11. _____	12. _____
13. _____	.01	14. _____
15. _____	16. _____	$4\frac{1}{5}$
17. _____	18. _____	$\frac{1}{200}$
100%	19. _____	20. _____

Find the percent, part, or whole in the following problems.

21. 35% of what is 311.50? _____

22. What is 17% of 98? _____

23. 7 is what percent of 350? _____

24. 225% of what is 795? _____

25. What is $\frac{1}{2}\%$ of 7700? _____

26. 17 is what percent of 51? _____

27. 26 is 66% of what? _____

28. What is 75% of 50? _____

29. $\frac{1}{4}$ is what percent of 5? _____

30. 150 is what percent of 30? _____

Solve.

31. Norma made 150 phone calls for her job as a salesperson. 5% of the people she called refused to speak with her. How many would talk with her? _____

32. Early on election night 1595 votes had been counted. That was 55% of the total. What was the total number of votes? _____

33. Dick just got a raise. His old salary was $4.25 an hour. His new salary is $4.76 an hour. His new salary is what percent of his old one? _____

Find the interest on the following.

34. $1000 at $5\frac{1}{4}$% for one year

_____

35. $3450 at 6.5% for four years

_____

36. $298 at 12% for six months

_____

37. $5600 at 4% for 3 years and 3 months

_____

38. $1000 at $7\frac{3}{4}$% for one year

_____

39. $3450 at 6.5% for eight years

_____

40. $298 at 15% for six months

_____

41. $560 at 4% for 3 years and 3 months

_____

Solve.

42. Ten-speed bikes are on sale at Bill's Bike World for $200.00. The original price was $240.00. What is the percent of decrease in the price of the bikes? _____

43. The rent on Kee Chan's apartment has been raised from $195.00 to $224.25 a month. What is the percent of increase in the rent? _____

44. The cost of a steak dinner at the Fireside has been raised from $6.50 to $7.80. That is an increase of what percent? _____

45. The Termans' monthly electric bills were $16.00 in the winter and $13.00 in the summer. What is the percent of decrease in their electric bills in the summer? _____

46. Jess bought a $150 tape recorder for 10% down and $13.25 a month for a year. What was the down payment? _____

47. What were the total monthly payments? _____

48. What was the total amount he paid for the tape recorder? _____

KEY/Lesson 17   1–20   Lesson 23   34, 38
Lesson 19   21, 24, 27, 32   Lesson 24   35–37, 39–41
Lesson 20   22, 25, 28, 31   Lesson 25   46–48
Lesson 21   23, 26, 29, 30   Lesson 26   33, 42–45

62

Part 1 test

Find the missing information.

	Percent		Decimal		Fraction
1.	_____	**2.**	_____		$\frac{1}{2}$
	16%	**3.**	_____	**4.**	_____
5.	_____		.75	**6.**	_____
7.	_____		9.21	**8.**	_____
9.	_____	**10.**	_____		$\frac{2}{3}$
11.	_____		.95	**12.**	_____
13.	_____	**14.**	_____		$\frac{1}{3}$
15.	_____		.83	**16.**	_____
	14%	**17.**	_____	**18.**	_____
	$\frac{1}{2}$%	**19.**	_____	**20.**	_____

Find the percent, part, or whole for the following problems.

21. 527 is what percent of 62? _____

22. 57% of 1000 equals what? _____

23. $8\frac{1}{3}$% of what is 144? _____

24. 42 is what percent of 126? _____

25. $16\frac{2}{3}$% of what is 366? _____

26. $\frac{1}{2}$ is what percent of $\frac{3}{4}$? _____

27. .75% of .5 is what? _____

28. 75% of 9650 is what? _____

29. 50% of the total vote was counted in District One. 1978 people in District One voted that day. How many of the ballots have been counted? _____

30. Tom's teenage son Jim pays 85% of the cost of his clothes, transportation, and entertainment. That amounts to all of his weekly pay, $30.00, from his part-time job. What is the amount of Jim's weekly expenses? _____

31. The cost of a bus ride is 55¢. The price is being raised a nickel. What percent is that of the old price? _____

Find the interest for the following problems.

32. a car loan of $2600 at 12% for 2 years

_____

33. a loan of $960 at $8\frac{1}{2}$% for 2 years and 9 months

_____

34. a home improvement loan of $16,570 at $10\frac{1}{2}$% for 10 years

_____

35. a furniture loan for $500 at 9.75% for four months

_____

Find the correct amounts for the blanks in these sentences.

36. "Color TVs have been marked down from $450 to $375," said Carol. "That's a _____% discount." _____

37. "They have an installment plan that lets me put $24.75 down and pay only $34.40 a month for a year," Carol added. "The down payment is _____% of the sale price." _____

38. "Wait a second," said her friend Marge. "That's $_____, all totalled." _____

39. "Oh," said Carol sadly, "then that's an increase of _____% over the sale price." _____

40. "Well, have you thought about getting a personal loan from the bank?" Marge asked. "$375 at 14% for 1 year would cost $_____." _____

41. "That is a total cost of $_____ for the bank loan," Carol said. _____

42. "The difference between the total cost of the installment loan and the total cost of the bank loan is $_____," said Marge. _____

KEY/Lesson 17   1–20
Lesson 19   23, 25, 28, 30   Lesson 23   40, 41
Lesson 20   22, 27, 29   Lesson 24   32–35
Lesson 21   21, 24, 26, 31   Lesson 25   37, 38, 42
                                Lesson 26   36, 39

66

Proportion, graphs, and measurement

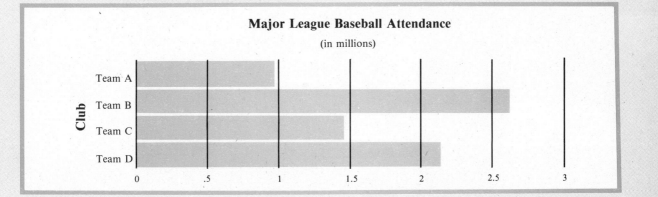

Major League Baseball Attendance

(in millions)

Pretest/Unit 6
Ratio and proportion

Solve the following proportion problems.

1. $\dfrac{5}{7} = \dfrac{n}{105}$ $n = $ _____

2. $\dfrac{17}{n} = \dfrac{21}{63}$ $n = $ _____

3. $\dfrac{\frac{1}{3}}{3} = \dfrac{n}{6}$ $n = $ _____

4. $\dfrac{.25}{2} = \dfrac{.75}{n}$ $n = $ _____

5. $\dfrac{99}{198} = \dfrac{n}{396}$ $n = $ _____

6. $\dfrac{\frac{1}{6}}{4} = \dfrac{n}{24}$ $n = $ _____

Fill in the space under the letter of the correct answer to each problem.

7. Mitchell Price works as a hair dresser. He can take care of 9 customers in 4 hours. How is that written as a ratio?

   a. $\dfrac{4}{9}$ b. $\dfrac{9}{4}$ c. $2\frac{1}{4}$ d. 4:9

8. He earns $.50 in tips for every $5.00 a customer spends in the shop. At the end of one week, his customers spent $225.00. How is the proportion written that will tell what he earned in tips?

   a. $\dfrac{\$5.00}{\$.50} = \dfrac{\$225}{n}$ b. $\dfrac{\$5.00}{n} = \dfrac{\$.50}{\$225}$ c. $\dfrac{1}{10} = \dfrac{n}{225}$ d. $\dfrac{10}{1} = \dfrac{n}{225}$

9. Three out of every 7 women will have a haircut as well as a shampoo. If 91 women come into the shop for a shampoo, how many will get their hair cut?

   a. 13   b. 21   c. 60   d. 39

10. The shop will pay Mitchell $2.00 in commission for every $5.00 he does in business. If he brings in $225 in one week, how much money will he get from the beauty shop?

    a. $90.00   b. $45.00   c. $9.00   d. $450.00

11. For every dollar he earns in wages, he earns two dollars in tips and commissions. At the end of the week his total income in tips and commissions was $112.50. What were his wages?

    a. $225.00   b. $56.25   c. $168.75   d. $115.50

Lesson 27
Writing ratios

A **ratio** shows the relationship between two numbers.
Here are three ways to write the ratio
5 policemen to 5000 people.

1. Use either **to** or **for**.

   5 policemen to 5000 people
   5 policemen for 5000 people

2. Use the ratio symbol (:).

   5 policemen : 5000 people

   Notice the first term in the problem is written first when the : is used.

3. Use the fraction method.

   $\dfrac{5 \text{ policemen}}{5000 \text{ people}}$ Notice the first term in the problem is written on top when the fraction method is used.

   Remember:
   Ratios must always have two numbers.
   Never write a ratio as a mixed number.

When a ratio is written as a fraction, it can be reduced.

$\dfrac{5 \text{ policemen}}{5000 \text{ people}}$ reduces to $\dfrac{1 \text{ policeman}}{1000 \text{ people}}$

A.
Write the ratio 24 chairs to 6 tables using the three different methods.

     24 chairs to 6 tables

     24 chairs : 6 tables

     $\dfrac{24 \text{ chairs}}{6 \text{ tables}}$ or $\dfrac{4 \text{ chairs}}{1 \text{ table}}$

B.
Write the ratio 25 students per teacher using the : and fraction methods.

The words **a, an, each,** or **per** used before a person or thing mean **one** person or thing.

     25 students : 1 teacher

     $\dfrac{25 \text{ students}}{1 \text{ teacher}}$

Objective/Write ratios from words.

Write these ratios using the : method.

1. two TVs to one household

_____

2. one accident to 10,000,000 miles flown

_____

3. one inch on a map to 25 miles

_____

4. 25 miles per gallon

_____

5. 8 ounces of meat for each person

_____

6. 24 boxes to a crate

_____

7. 20 parts alcohol to 80 parts gasoline

_____

8. one post for every 3 feet of fence

_____

Write these ratios using the fraction method.

9. 125 people to 275 seats on a plane

_____

10. 5 inches on a map for 65 miles

_____

11. driving 336 miles in 6 hours

_____

12. 2 quarts of cleaner to 5 quarts of water

_____

13. 3 yards of cloth for each dress

_____

14. 24 cases of nails to 1284 pounds

_____

15. reading 45 pages in 55 minutes

_____

Objective/Write ratios from words.

Lesson 28
Writing proportions

A proportion is a statement that two ratios are equal. Proportions can be written in two ways:

$6:8::3:4$ This proportion is read, 6 is to 8 as 3 is to 4.

or

$$\frac{6}{8} = \frac{3}{4}$$

Notice the proportion symbol (::).

A.

Write the proportion
1 is to 2 as 8 is to 16.

$$\frac{1}{2} = \frac{8}{16} \quad \text{or} \quad 1:2 :: 8:16$$

B.

Write the proportion
2 is to 3 as 34 is to 51.

$$\frac{2}{3} = \frac{34}{51} \quad \text{or} \quad 2:3 :: 34:51$$

C.

Write the proportion
108 is to 12 as 27 is to 3.

$$\frac{108}{12} = \frac{27}{3} \quad \text{or} \quad 108:12 :: 27:3$$

Write the following proportions using both methods.

1. 12 is to 18 as 44 is to 66

   _____ _____

2. 27 is to 54 as 45 is to 90

   _____ _____

3. 9 is to 81 as 15 is to 135

   _____ _____

4. 10 is to 100 as 100 is to 1000

   _____ _____

5. 150 is to 300 as 75 is to 150

   _____ _____

6. 99 is to 1 as 990 is to 10

   _____ _____

7. 348 is to 58 as 162 is to 27

   _____ _____

8. 17 is to 51 as 1 is to 3

   _____ _____

9. 55 is to 200 as 110 is to 400

   _____ _____

Lesson 29
Solving proportions

These are the **cross-products** in a proportion.
The cross products are equal.

$\dfrac{6}{8} = \dfrac{3}{4}$ $6 \times 4 = 24$

$\dfrac{6}{8} = \dfrac{3}{4}$ $8 \times 3 = 24$

$\dfrac{3}{4} = \dfrac{9}{12}$ $4 \times 9 = 36$
$3 \times 12 = 36$

Check these proportions to see if their cross-products are equal.

$\dfrac{15}{45} = \dfrac{17}{51}$ $15 \times 51 = ?$
$45 \times 17 = ?$

$\dfrac{2}{9} = \dfrac{18}{81}$ $2 \times 81 = ?$
$9 \times 18 = ?$

To solve a proportion means to find a missing number in the proportion. Use these rules:
1. Let the letter n stand for the missing number.
2. Find the cross-product of the numbers you know.
3. Divide the cross-product by the number that is left.

A.

$\dfrac{3}{4} = \dfrac{n}{16}$ $\dfrac{3 \times 16}{4} = \dfrac{48}{4} = 12$

$n = 12$

B.

$\dfrac{7}{n} = \dfrac{35}{50}$ $\dfrac{7 \times 50}{35} = \dfrac{350}{35} = 10$

$n = 10$

C.

$\dfrac{n}{8} = \dfrac{30}{48}$ $\dfrac{8 \times 30}{48} = \dfrac{240}{48} = 5$

$n = 5$

D.

$\dfrac{9}{14} = \dfrac{45}{n}$ $\dfrac{14 \times 45}{9} = \dfrac{630}{9} = 70$

$n = 70$

Objective/Use cross-products to solve proportions.

E.

Solve the proportion in this word problem.

26 egg cartons fit inside a cardboard box.
How many cardboard boxes will be needed for 3900 egg cartons?

1. Set up the proportion with equal ratios. Let n be the missing number.

   Use the ratio $\dfrac{\text{egg cartons}}{\text{cardboard boxes}}.$ $\dfrac{26}{1} = \dfrac{3900}{n}$

2. Solve using cross-products.

   $\dfrac{1 \times 3900}{26} = 150$ $n = 150$ cardboard boxes

---

Solve each problem using proportions.

1. A town wants to keep its ratio of 7 small parks to 5000 people. If the town grows to 15,000, how many parks will it need?

   _____

2. José used 22 gallons of gasoline on his 550-mile tour of Nova Scotia. How much gasoline will he need for a 320-mile trip?

   _____

3. If a plane flies 932 miles in 2 hours, how far will it fly in 7 hours?

   _____

4. Rudy must make 23 radio parts in 40 minutes at work. How many will he make by the end of an 8-hour day?

   _____

5. Three cooks can produce meals for 27 people an evening. The restaurant expands to seat 40. How many new cooks should be hired?

   _____

6. 850 pancakes were served to 300 people at the first sitting of the pancake dinner. 220 tickets have been bought for the second sitting. How many pancakes will probably be eaten by those 220 people?

   _____

For extra practice see pages 149 and 150.

0   5   6

Objective/Use cross-products to solve proportions.

Life skill
Finding prices by proportion

Rules:
1. Write a proportion.
2. Solve for *n*.
3. Round up to the next penny if there is a remainder.

2 bags of carrots $.98   **4 cans of beets $1.07**

A.
What is the cost of 1 bag of carrots?

$$\frac{2}{\$.98} = \frac{1}{n} \qquad \frac{\$.98 \times 1}{2} = \$.49$$

$$n = \$.49$$

B.
What is the cost of 3 cans of beets?

$$\frac{4}{\$1.07} = \frac{3}{n} \qquad \frac{\$1.07 \times 3}{4} = \$.80\frac{1}{4}$$

$$n = \$.81$$

Solve the problems using these prices.

5 pounds of potatoes for $1.00
2 heads of lettuce for $1.44
3 cans of tomatoes for $1.71
6 ounces of bean sprouts for $.66

3 bags of candy for $2.73
4 cans of soup for $1.64
2 pounds of hamburger for $3.28

1. What is the cost of 10 pounds of potatoes?   _____

2. What would 3 heads of lettuce cost?   _____

3. What would nine cans of tomatoes cost?   _____

4. How much would 18 ounces of bean sprouts cost?   _____

5. How much would 2 cans of soup cost?   _____

6. What would be the cost of 2 pounds of potatoes?   _____

7. What would 3 pounds of hamburger cost?   _____

8. What would sixteen cans of soup cost?   _____

9. What is the cost of four bags of candy?   _____

Lesson 30
Proportions with fractions and mixed numbers

You can write proportions using fractions or mixed numbers if you are careful about numerators and denominators. Always convert mixed numbers to improper fractions before solving the proportion. It may be easier to solve the proportion in two steps, as below.

A.

One-half cup of flour is used for a recipe that makes 4 servings. How much flour is needed to make 12 servings?

$$\frac{\frac{1}{2}}{4} = \frac{n}{12}$$

Find the cross-product: $\frac{1}{2} \times \frac{12}{1} = 6$

Divide: $6 \div 4 = \frac{6}{1} \times \frac{1}{4} = \frac{3}{2} = 1\frac{1}{2}$

Answer: $n = 1\frac{1}{2}$ cups of flour

B.

Maine had rain 4 times in 30 days, for a total of $13\frac{1}{2}$ inches. What was the average rainfall per day for that period? (Find the total of the group of numbers. Divide by the number of numbers that made the total.)

$$\frac{13\frac{1}{2} \text{ in.}}{30 \text{ days}} = \frac{n}{1 \text{ day}}$$

Change the mixed number to an improper fraction.

$$\frac{\frac{27}{2}}{30} = \frac{n}{1}$$

Find the cross-product: $\frac{27}{2} \times 1 = \frac{27}{2}$

Divide: $\frac{27}{2} \div 30 = \frac{27}{60} = .45$

Answer: $n = .45$ inch
The average rainfall was $\frac{.45 \text{ in.}}{\text{day}}$

Solve the following proportions.

1. $\dfrac{\frac{1}{3}}{12} = \dfrac{n}{9}$ _____

2. $\dfrac{\frac{1}{8}}{88} = \dfrac{11}{n}$ _____

3. $\dfrac{\frac{3}{4}}{n} = \dfrac{6\frac{3}{4}}{1800}$ _____

4. $\dfrac{n}{8} = \dfrac{\frac{3}{8}}{4}$ _____

5. $\dfrac{5.25}{10} = \dfrac{n}{25}$ _____

6. $\dfrac{11}{3} = \dfrac{n}{\frac{1}{6}}$ _____

Objective/Solve proportions with fractions and mixed numbers.

0   5   6

Life skill
Reading a map

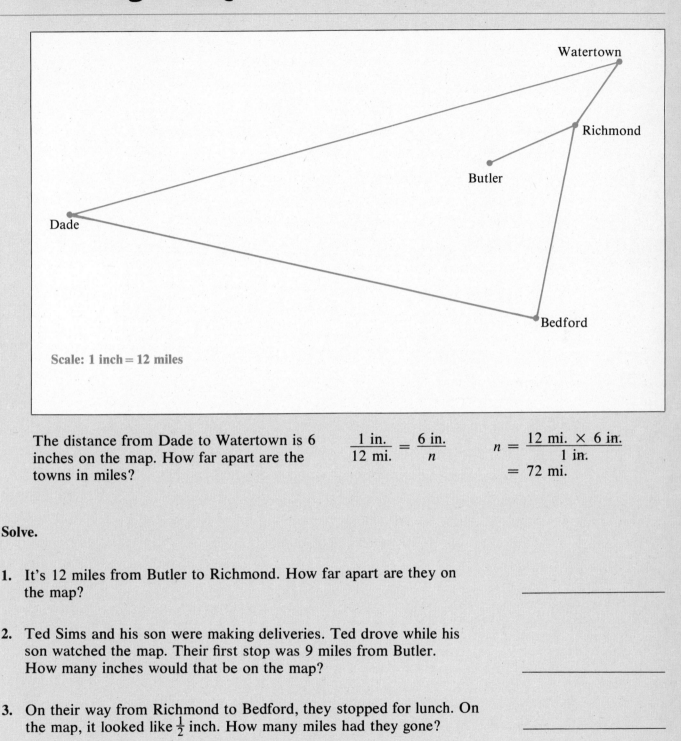

Watertown

Richmond

Butler

Dade

Bedford

Scale: 1 inch = 12 miles

The distance from Dade to Watertown is 6 inches on the map. How far apart are the towns in miles?

$$\frac{1 \text{ in.}}{12 \text{ mi.}} = \frac{6 \text{ in.}}{n}$$

$$n = \frac{12 \text{ mi.} \times 6 \text{ in.}}{1 \text{ in.}}$$
$$= 72 \text{ mi.}$$

Solve.

1. It's 12 miles from Butler to Richmond. How far apart are they on the map? _____

2. Ted Sims and his son were making deliveries. Ted drove while his son watched the map. Their first stop was 9 miles from Butler. How many inches would that be on the map? _____

3. On their way from Richmond to Bedford, they stopped for lunch. On the map, it looked like $\frac{1}{2}$ inch. How many miles had they gone? _____

4. A tire went flat just as they crossed the Shepaug River. On the map, the river crossed the road $\frac{5}{8}$ inch away from Bedford. How far away from the town were they? _____

Objective/Use proportions to figure distance.

Life skill
Changing a recipe

Spaghetti/4 servings

Brown in a heavy pot $\frac{1}{2}$ pound sausage
$\frac{1}{3}$ pound hamburger
4 tablespoons chopped onion

Add   3 ounces tomato paste
8 ounces tomato sauce
16 ounces canned whole tomatoes
1 teaspoon sugar
$1\frac{1}{2}$ teaspoons salt
$\frac{1}{2}$ teaspoon basil
2 teaspoons oregano

Simmer 2 hours.
Serve over 1 pound of boiled spaghetti noodles.

If the Khedroos need only 3 servings, how much of each ingredient should they use?

The Franklins want to cook enough for 10 servings. How much of each ingredient do they need?

1. Sausage	_____	11. Sausage	_____
2. Hamburger	_____	12. Hamburger	_____
3. Onion	_____	13. Onion	_____
4. Tomato paste	_____	14. Tomato paste	_____
5. Tomato sauce	_____	15. Tomato sauce	_____
6. Whole tomatoes	_____	16. Whole tomatoes	_____
7. Sugar	_____	17. Sugar	_____
8. Salt	_____	18. Salt	_____
9. Basil	_____	19. Basil	_____
10. Oregano	_____	20. Oregano	_____

Objective/Use proportions to convert recipes.

Posttest/Unit 6

Solve the following proportion problems.

1. $\dfrac{7}{98} = \dfrac{n}{70}$ $n =$ _____

4. $\dfrac{n}{.5} = \dfrac{15}{75}$ $n =$ _____

2. $\dfrac{2}{5} = \dfrac{50}{n}$ $n =$ _____

5. $\dfrac{53}{n} = \dfrac{33}{66}$ $n =$ _____

3. $\dfrac{\frac{1}{2}}{\frac{1}{4}} = \dfrac{n}{\frac{3}{4}}$ $n =$ _____

6. $\dfrac{\frac{3}{5}}{7} = \dfrac{n}{35}$ $n =$ _____

Fill in the space under the letter of the correct answer to each problem.

7. Cal Adams works in a warehouse. He packed 63 cartons in the last 3 crates on hand. He has 1395 more cartons to pack. How many more crates does he need?

a	b	c	d
||	||	||	||

   a. 67   **b.** 45   **c.** 4.5   **d.** 225

8. In 4 hours he will pack 18 crates. How many crates will he pack in 6 hours?

a	b	c	d
||	||	||	||

   a. 108   **b.** 24   **c.** $4\frac{1}{2}$ **d.** 27

9. Seven crates fit on a platform. Each platform weighs 420 pounds. How much will 98 crates weigh?

   a. 60 pounds
   b. 5880 pounds
   c. 686 pounds
   d. 40,160 pounds

a	b	c	d
||	||	||	||

10. Hector works three hours overtime for every 40 hours on the job. How many hours of overtime will he work at the end of 240 hours on the job?

a	b	c	d
||	||	||	||

   a. 120   **b.** 6   **c.** 18   **d.** $16\frac{2}{3}$

11. He earns $6.20 an hour. He earns time-and-a-half for overtime. What is his hourly overtime pay?

a	b	c	d
||	||	||	||

   a. $9.30   **b.** $12.40   **c.** $3.10   **d.** $6.51

Percent of population employed in different industries

Total: 80,252,000 employees

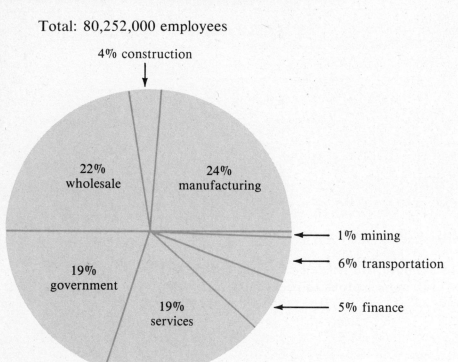

4% construction

22% wholesale

24% manufacturing

1% mining

6% transportation

19% government

19% services

5% finance

1. What percent of the workers are in transportation? _____

2. What percent of the workers are in mining? _____

3. How many people work in wholesale? _____

4. How many people work in government? _____

5. What is the ratio between the percent of people working in construction and the percent of people working in manufacturing? _____

6. What is the difference between the number of people working in wholesale and the number of people working in finance? _____

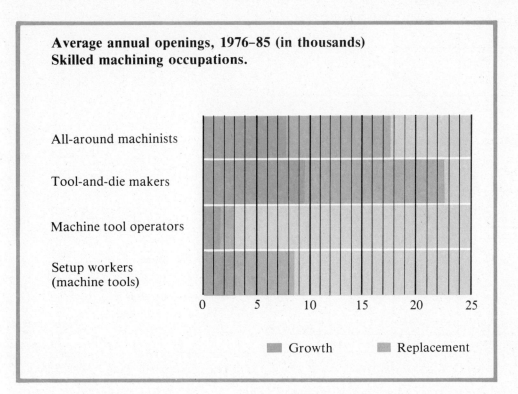

Average annual openings, 1976–85 (in thousands)
Skilled machining occupations.

All-around machinists

Tool-and-die makers

Machine tool operators

Setup workers
(machine tools)

0   5   10   15   20   25

■ Growth   ■ Replacement

This **horizontal bar graph** shows that the average number of all-around machinists for the years 1976-85 is 17,600. Of these, about 7,600 are new openings and 10,000 are replacements of people now working.

7. In a year, about how many new tool-and-die maker jobs will be created?

_____

8. About how many tool-and-die makers are needed as replacements in a year?

_____

9. How many new and replacement setup workers will be needed in a year?

_____

10. How many replacements will be needed for machine tool operators?

_____

11. The total number of openings for setup workers per year is about what percent of the total number of openings for tool-and-die makers?

_____

12. What is the ratio of new jobs to replacement positions for all-around machinists in a year?

_____

Size of labor force by sex, 1950-1990

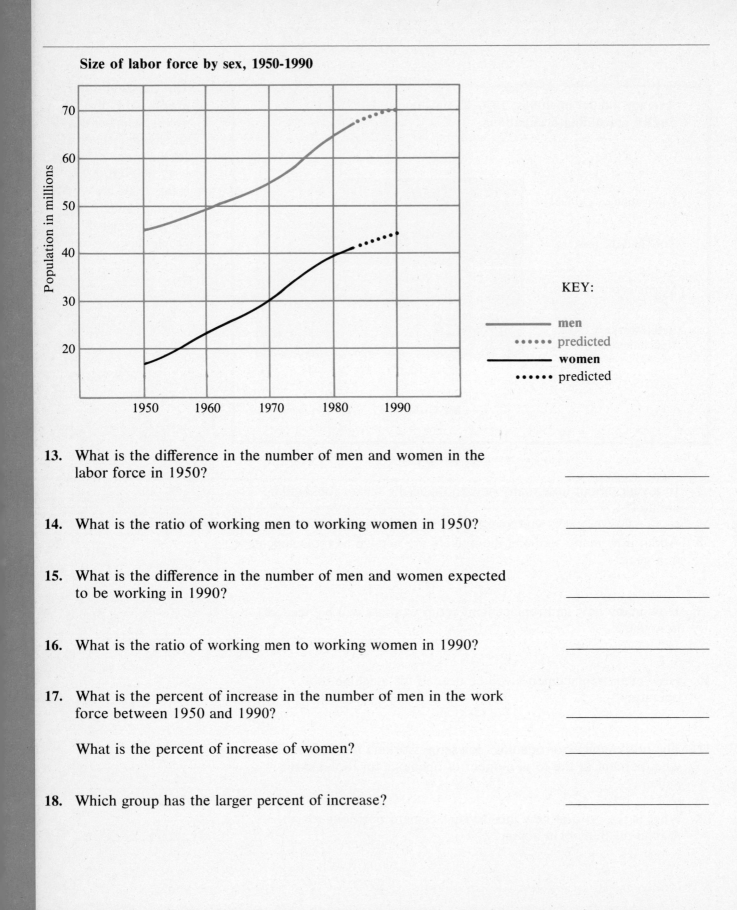

13. What is the difference in the number of men and women in the labor force in 1950?

_____

14. What is the ratio of working men to working women in 1950?

_____

15. What is the difference in the number of men and women expected to be working in 1990?

_____

16. What is the ratio of working men to working women in 1990?

_____

17. What is the percent of increase in the number of men in the work force between 1950 and 1990?

_____

   What is the percent of increase of women?

_____

18. Which group has the larger percent of increase?

_____

Lesson 31
Reading a circle graph

The Parks' budget of $9500 by percent

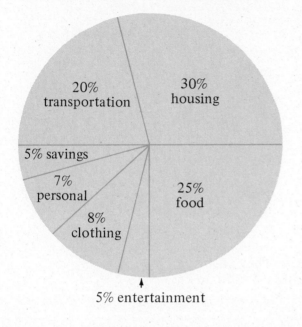

20% transportation

30% housing

5% savings

7% personal

8% clothing

25% food

5% entertainment

The circle graph represents 100% of an amount.

The graph is divided into parts. Each part represents some percent of the whole amount.

The sum of the part percents is 100%.

5% of the total income went to savings.

$$5\% \text{ of } \$9500 = .05 \times \$9500$$
$$= \$475.00$$

Checklist:
1. Always read the title.
2. Always read the name of each part and the percent it represents.

Find the answers by using the circle graph above.

1. What percent does the whole circle represent? _____

2. What percent of their income is allowed for housing? _____

3. What percent of their income is allowed for transportation? _____

4. How many dollars were allowed for food? _____

5. How many dollars were allowed for clothing? _____

6. How many dollars were allowed for personal purchases and entertainment? _____

7. What is the difference in dollars allowed for food and savings? _____

8. What is the ratio of the percent of money allowed for food to the percent allowed for housing? _____

9. The percent allowed for housing is how many times greater than the percent allowed for transportation? _____

10. How many times greater is the percent allowed for food than the percent allowed for savings? _____

The Browns' annual expenses by percent

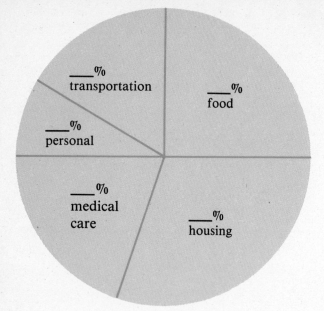

_____% transportation

_____% personal

_____% food

_____% medical care

_____% housing

The Browns earned a total of $6700 last year after taxes. They spent $2010 on housing, $1675 on food, $1005 on transportation, $1340 on medical care, and $670 on personal purchases.

Find what percent of their total income was used for each of these items. Place the answers in the correct space on the graph.

11. Housing   _____

12. Food   _____

13. Transportation   _____

14. Medical care   _____

15. Personal spending   _____

Objective/Read a circle graph.

The population of the United States in 1980: 221,800,000

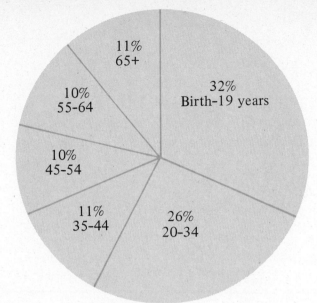

11%
65+

10%
55-64

10%
45-54

11%
35-44

32%
Birth–19 years

26%
20-34

16. What was the total population of the U.S. in 1980? _____

17. What two things are being compared in this graph? _____

_____

18. What percent of the population was between the ages of 20 and 34? _____

19. What percent of the population was between 45 and 54? _____

20. Which age group was the largest? _____

21. Which two age groups were the smallest? _____

22. Which other two age groups were equal in size? _____

23. How many people were less than 20 years old? _____

24. How many people were between 20 and 34 years old? _____

25. How many people were over 65? _____

For extra practice see page 151.

0   20   25

Objective/Read a circle graph.

Lesson 32
Reading a picture graph

Picture graphs compare information by using symbols.
A **symbol** is a picture that stands for something.
The **key** is usually near the graph. It tells you what the symbols in the
graph stand for.

Checklist:
1. Always read the title of the graph.
2. Always decide what things are being compared.
3. Always look at the key to see what the symbol stands for.

The number of people completing 12 years of school
in 1960, 1970, and 1980.

1960	1,864,000	
1970	2,906,000	
1980	2,756,600	

Key: ▐ = 100,000 people

Find the information from the picture graph above.

1. What are the three years being compared?

_____

2. Each symbol represents _____ people.

How many people completed 12 years of
school in:

3. 1960?   _____

4. 1970?   _____

5. 1980?   _____

6. What is the ratio of people graduating in
1960 to 1970?

_____

7. The number of 1980 graduates is what
percent of the 1960 graduates?

_____

8. What is the ratio of people who completed
12th grade in 1980 to those in 1960?

_____

Objective/Read a picture graph.

Average lifetime income according to years of education

Less than 8 years	$$$$$	*Key:* $ = $100,000
Complete 8 years	$$$$$$$	
High school 9–11 years	$$$$$$$$	
Complete 12 years	$$$$$$$$$	
College 1–3 years	$$$$$$$$$$$	
College 4 years	$$$$$$$$$$$$	

9. What does the symbol $ stand for?

_____

10. On the average how much money will a person who has attended 11 years of school earn in a lifetime?

_____

11. On the average how much money will a person who has completed 12 years of school earn in a lifetime?

_____

12. On the average how much money will a person who has completed 8 years of school earn in a lifetime?

_____

13. What is the difference in average lifetime income between a person completing 8th grade and a person completing 11th grade?

_____

14. What is the ratio of average income between a person completing 12th grade and a person completing college?

_____

15. The average income of a person who completes 12 years of school is what percent of the average income of a person who completes 10 years of school?

_____

16. What is the difference in average earnings between those completing 11 and 12 years of school?

_____

Lesson 33
Reading a bar graph

Average family income by years

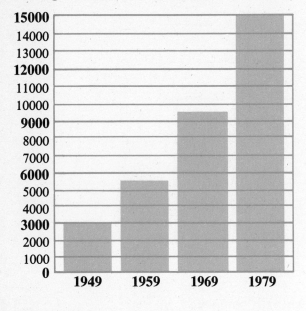

Checklist:
1. Always read the title.
2. Decide what things are being compared.
3. Look to see if there is a key for symbols.
4. Check to see how the numbers change: by 10s, 100s, 1000s, 10,000s.

A.

What was the average family income in 1949?

1. Find the year 1949.
2. Read to the end of the bar.
3. Draw a line straight across to the income.
4. It reads $3000 average family income.

B.

What was the average family income in 1959?

1. Find 1959 on the graph.
2. Read to the end of the bar.
3. Draw a line from the end of the bar straight across to the income.
4. The line does not end at an even number. It is more than halfway between 5000 and 6000. Now you have to guess.
5. It is about $\frac{6}{10}$ of the way between the two numbers.

$$\frac{6}{10} \text{ of } 1000 = \frac{6}{10} \times \frac{1000}{1} = 600$$

6. The average family income in 1959 was about $5000 + $600 = $5600.

Solve these problems. Round off to the nearest whole percent.

1. What was the average income for 1969? _____

2. What was the average income for 1979? _____

3. What is the difference in average income between 1949 and 1959? _____

4. What is the difference between the average income in 1959 and 1969? _____

5. The average income for 1979 is what percent of the average income for 1949? _____

6. What is the ratio of the average 1979 income to the average 1949 income? _____

Objective/Read bar graphs.

Income of men and women at different jobs in industry and business.

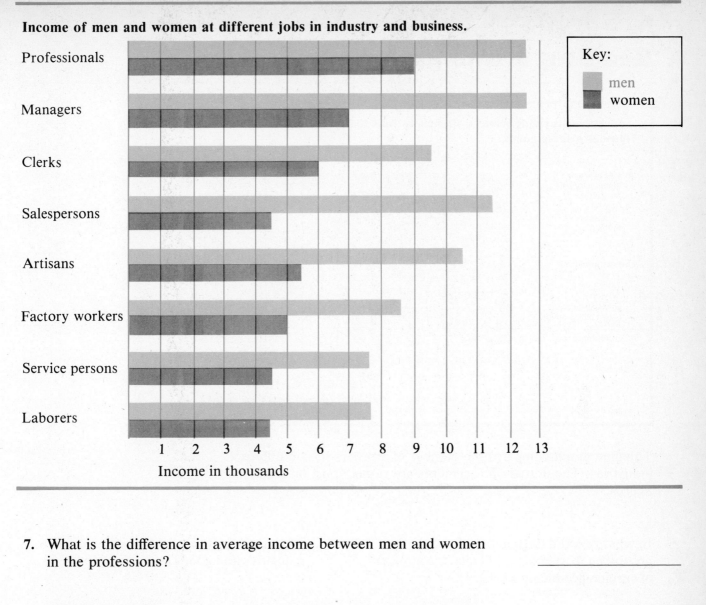

Key:
men
women

Income in thousands

Professionals
Managers
Clerks
Salespersons
Artisans
Factory workers
Service persons
Laborers

1 2 3 4 5 6 7 8 9 10 11 12 13

7. What is the difference in average income between men and women in the professions?

_____

8. What is the difference in average income between men and women in service jobs?

_____

9. Which job has the greatest difference in average income between the two groups?

_____

10. Women's average income in the clerical field is what percent of men's clerical pay?

_____

11. Women's average income in labor jobs is what percent of men's in those jobs?

_____

12. Women's salaries in the professions are what percent of men's?

_____

For extra practice see pages 152 and 153.

0   10   12

Objective/Read bar graphs.

Lesson 34
Reading a line graph

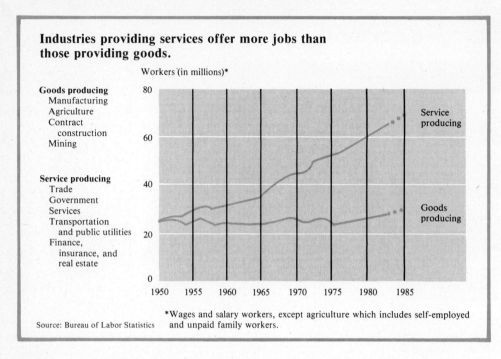

Industries providing services offer more jobs than those providing goods.

Workers (in millions)*

Goods producing
Manufacturing
Agriculture
Contract
    construction
Mining

Service producing
Trade
Government
Services
Transportation
    and public utilities
Finance,
    insurance, and
    real estate

Service producing

Goods producing

1950 1955 1960 1965 1970 1975 1980 1985

*Wages and salary workers, except agriculture which includes self-employed
and unpaid family workers.
Source: Bureau of Labor Statistics

This line graph compares the number of workers in two different industries. The dotted-line segments are projections, or predicted figures.

A.

In what year did the number of goods-producing workers almost equal the number of service-producing workers?

1. Find the line that shows the service-producing industry.
2. Find the line that shows the goods-producing industry.
3. Find the point where the lines are closest together.
4. Draw a vertical line down to the the year.

Answer: 1950

Checklist:
1. Always read the title.
2. Decide what things are being compared.
3. Look for a key for symbols.
4. Check to see how the numbers change: by 10s, 100s, 1000s, or 10,000s.
5. Always read the lines from left to right.

B.

What is the projected ratio between service industries and goods industries for 1985?

1. Find the line that shows the service-producing industry.
2. Find the line that shows the goods-producing industry.
3. Draw a vertical line from 1985 to the lines for each industry.
4. Draw a horizontal line straight across to the number of workers in each industry.

Answer: $\dfrac{70 \text{ million}}{30 \text{ million}}$

Vocabulary:
A **projection,** or projected figure, is a guess based on past figures.
Vertical means up and down.
Horizontal means across.

Objective/Read line graphs.

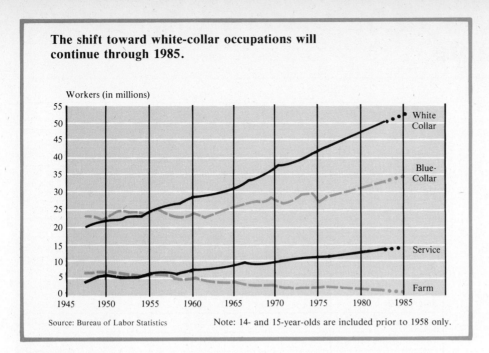

The shift toward white-collar occupations will continue through 1985.

Workers (in millions)

White Collar

Blue-Collar

Service

Farm

1945 1950 1955 1960 1965 1970 1975 1980 1985

Source: Bureau of Labor Statistics   Note: 14- and 15-year-olds are included prior to 1958 only.

Solve.

1. Which group has decreased in number over the years? _____

2. What is the difference in the number of farm workers between 1950 and 1985? _____

3. What is the percent of decrease? _____

4. What is the approximate difference between the number of service workers and blue-collar workers in 1970? _____

5. What is the percent of increase between 1950 and 1985 for white-collar workers? _____

6. What is the average percent of increase per year for white-collar workers in this 35-year period? _____

7. What is the difference in the number of blue-collar workers between 1950 and 1985? _____

8. What is the percent of increase? _____

9. What is the average percent of increase per year for blue-collar workers in this 35-year period? _____

0   7   9

Objective/Read line graphs.

Lesson 35
Reading a table

The two tables list long-distance phone costs for dial-direct and operator-assisted calls.

There are three types of dial-direct charges and two types of operator-assisted charges.

All charges are given in dollars.

To find the cost of a call, first decide if you can dial directly or if you need operator assistance.

Then decide on the time of the call.

Find the cost of a one-minute, dial-direct call from Chicago to Seattle made in the evening.

Read down the dial-direct column for evening rates.

Read across the row from Seattle.

The column and row intersect (cross) at the cost, $.38.

For an operator-assisted call, follow the same steps but add operator-assisted charges to the total.

Checklist:
1. Read the title.
2. Read the vertical subjects.
3. Read the horizontal subjects.
4. Decide what the numbers inside the chart mean.

DIAL-DIRECT

sample rates from Chicago to:	WEEKDAY full rate		EVENING 40% discount		NIGHT & WEEKEND 60% discount	
	First Minute	Each Additional Minute	First Minute	Each Additional Minute	First Minute	Each Additional Minute
Atlanta, Ga.	.62	.43	.38	.26	.25	.18
Boston, Mass.	.62	.43	.38	.26	.25	.18
Denver, Colo.	.62	.43	.38	.26	.25	.18
Detroit, Mich.	.58	.39	.35	.24	.24	.16
Los Angeles, Cal.	.64	.44	.39	.27	.26	.18
Miami, Fla.	.64	.44	.39	.27	.26	.18
Milwaukee, Wis.	.57	.37	.35	.23	.23	.15
Minneapolis, Minn.	.59	.42	.36	.26	.24	.17
New Orleans, La.	.62	.43	.38	.26	.25	.18
New York, N.Y.	.62	.43	.38	.26	.25	.18
Seattle, Wash.	.64	.44	.38	.27	.25	.18
Washington, D.C.	.62	.43	.38	.26	.25	.18

Rates in effect October 1, 1983, and do not include tax charges.

OPERATOR-ASSISTED [*]

STATION-TO-STATION		PERSON-TO-PERSON
1-10 miles	$ .75	$3.00 all mileages
11-22 miles	1.10	
23-3000 miles	1.55	

[*]Note: Add to this base charge, minute rates from the above chart.

Objective/Read tables.

1. What are the two types of calls you can make?   _____

   _____

2. What are the three types of charges for a dial-direct call?   _____

   _____

   _____

3. What are the two types of charges for an operator-assisted call?   _____

   _____

4. What is the minimum amount of time for a dial-direct call?   _____

5. What is the minimum amount of time for an operator-assisted call?   _____

6. Do these charges include taxes?   _____

7. What is the difference in price between a 3-minute, dial-direct evening call and a 3-minute, operator-assisted, station-to-station evening call, to Miami?   _____

8. What is the difference in price between a 3-minute, operator-assisted, station-to-station call to Denver and a 3-minute, person-to-person call to Denver?   _____

9. What is the price of a 7-minute operator-assisted phone call to New York, when you call station-to-station in the evening?   _____

10. What is the price of a 12-minute call to Miami, calling person-to-person on a Monday at 10 in the morning?   _____

11. What is the difference in cost between a 5-minute phone call to Los Angeles dialed directly on a Saturday, and a 5-minute operator-assisted call made station-to-station on a Wednesday afternoon?   _____

12. On a Thursday evening, what is the ratio of the cost of an operator-assisted, station-to-station call to New York to the cost of a person-to-person call to New York, for the first three minutes?   _____

Objective/Read tables.

The consumer price index shows the changing value of a dollar. The same amount of food cost $.75 in 1950, $.85 in 1957, $1.00 in 1967, and $1.92 in 1977.

Consumer price index				
Years	Budget items			
	Food	Housing	Clothes	Transportation
1950	$ .75	$ .70	$ .79	$ .49
1957	$ .85	$ .85	$ .87	$ .73
1967	$1.00	$1.00	$1.00	$1.00
1977	$1.92	$1.77	$1.78	$1.82

Find the answers.

13. What is the vertical subject? _____

14. What is the horizontal subject? _____

15. What do the numbers in the table represent? _____

16. What is the title of the table? _____

17. Food that cost $2.00 in 1967 would cost how much in 1977? _____

18. Food that cost $2.00 in 1967 would have cost how much in 1950? _____

19. What is the amount of increase in food prices from 1950 to 1977? _____

20. What is the difference in the price of transportation between 1957 and 1977? _____

21. 1977 food prices have increased by what percent over 1967 food prices? _____

22. 1977 clothes prices have increased by what percent over 1967 clothes prices? _____

23. What is the ratio of 1957 housing costs to 1967 housing costs? _____

Objective/Read tables.

0   18   23

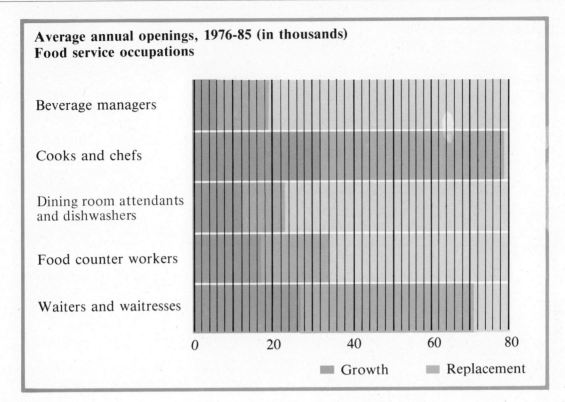

Average annual openings, 1976-85 (in thousands)
Food service occupations

Beverage managers

Cooks and chefs

Dining room attendants
and dishwashers

Food counter workers

Waiters and waitresses

0   20   40   60   80

■ Growth   ■ Replacement

Solve.

1. About how many new waiter/waitress openings will be created in a year? _____

2. About how many waiter/waitress openings per year are replacement openings? _____

3. What is the total number of waiter/waitress openings in a year? _____

4. What is the ratio between new and replacement openings for waiters and waitresses? _____

5. Which type of food service job needs the most people? _____

6. What is the ratio of the total number of cook/chef openings to the total number of waiter/waitress openings? _____

7. What percent of food counter worker openings are replacements? _____

8. What is the ratio of total food counter worker openings to total dining room attendant/dishwasher openings? _____

9. What is the difference between the number of waiter/waitress openings and the number of food counter worker openings? _____

Groups in the U.S. by percent (1980)
Total population: 226,505,000

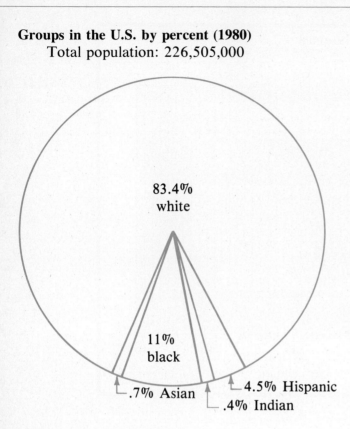

83.4%
white

11%
black

.7% Asian

4.5% Hispanic

.4% Indian

10. What type of graph is this? _____

11. How many people are black? _____

12. How many people are Hispanic? _____

13. How many people are Asian? _____

14. What is the ratio of blacks to whites? (Use the percent figures.) _____

15. What fraction of the population is Indian? (Find the ratio of Indians to the total population.) _____

16. What fraction of the population is Asian? _____

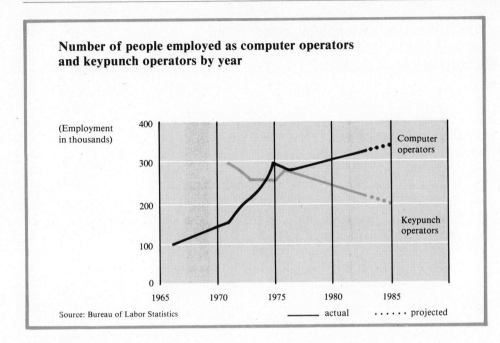

Number of people employed as computer operators and keypunch operators by year

(Employment in thousands)

Source: Bureau of Labor Statistics   ——— actual   · · · · · projected

17. In which 5-year period did the number of computer operators increase the most?

18. What is the difference between the number of people working as computer operators in 1970 and the number projected for 1985?

19. What is the difference between the number of keypunch operators in 1975 and the number projected for 1985?

20. What is the percent of increase projected for computer operators between 1970 and 1985?

21. What is the percent of decrease projected for keypunch operators between 1975 and 1985?

22. What is the projected ratio of computer operators to keypunch operators in 1985?

Pretest/Unit 8
Measurement

1. Joe needs a longer hose to finish installing a washing machine. If the one he has now is 4 m 27 cm long and he adds to it one that is 85 cm long, what will be the total length of the hose? _____

2. Sandy Johnson spilled seven ounces of sugar from a container holding 4 pounds 3 ounces. How much did he have left? _____

3. Three people were planning a fishing trip. To get to the lake was a drive of 12 hours 45 minutes. If each drove an equal number of hours, how long did each one drive? _____

4. How many liters of soup does Juanita need to serve 5 people 250 ml each? _____

5. Karen plans on putting up 4 gallons 1 quart of tomato sauce. How many jars will she need if each one holds 1 quart? _____

6. To make the chemical solution needed to develop film, Anita stirs 50 ml of developer into 100 ml of warm water and then adds water until she has 1 liter. How much more water must she add? _____

7. The package Mrs. Meger wanted to mail to the United States weighed 1 kg 230 g. The gift itself weighed 975 g. What did the packaging weigh? _____

8. The lumberyard sold boards exactly 2 yards long. José wanted 1 foot 2 inches sawed off. How long would the remaining piece of wood be? _____

Figure the price per unit and circle the better buy.

AAA   Hardware

Insulating stripping, 60¢ per meter

Paint thinner, 89¢ per liter

Chain link fencing, $17.50 per yard

Paint, $9.95 per gallon

BBB   Home Improvement Center

Insulating stripping, 20 meters for $11.00

Paint thinner, 800 ml for 65¢

Chain link fencing, $7.90 per foot

Paint, $3.05 per quart

AAA Hardware   BBB Home Improvement Center

9. Insulating stripping   10. Insulating stripping
    _____ per meter   _____ per meter

11. Paint thinner   12. Paint thinner
     _____ per *l*   _____ per *l*

13. Chain link fencing   14. Chain link fencing
     _____ per foot   _____ per foot

15. Paint   16. Paint
     _____ per quart   _____ per quart

Lesson 36
Introduction to measurement

These pictures compare similar metric and standard measurement units. Look at them carefully. Then answer the questions on the next page.

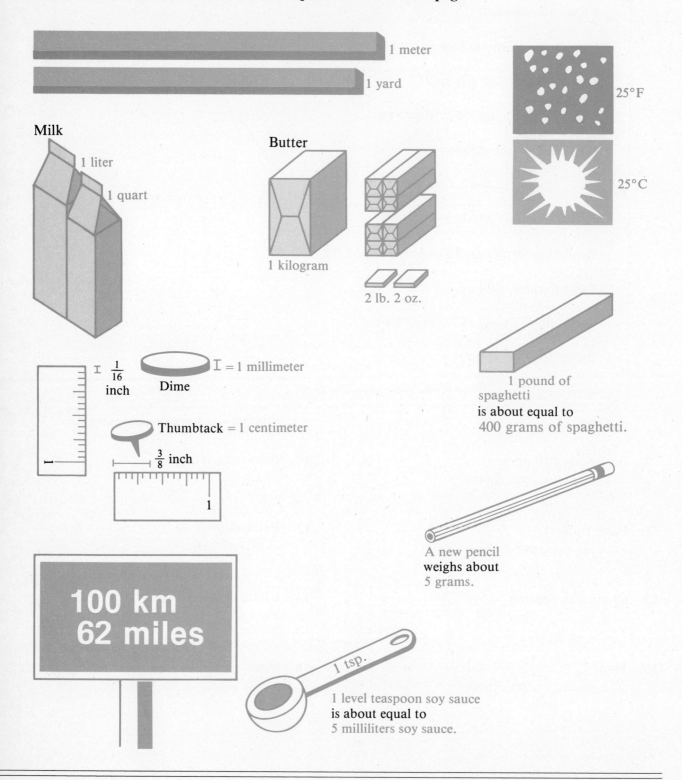

1 meter

1 yard

25°F

25°C

Milk

1 liter

1 quart

Butter

1 kilogram

2 lb. 2 oz.

$\frac{1}{16}$ inch

Dime

I = 1 millimeter

Thumbtack = 1 centimeter

$\frac{3}{8}$ inch

1

1 pound of spaghetti **is about equal to** 400 grams of spaghetti.

A new pencil **weighs about** 5 grams.

100 km
62 miles

1 tsp.

1 level teaspoon soy sauce **is about equal to** 5 milliliters soy sauce.

Objective/Understand measurements.

Use the drawings and your own experience to answer the following
questions. Decide what kind of measure is being used. Then put the letter
of the correct measure in the blank.

    A. Weight measure
    B. Volume measure
    C. Length measure

1. grams	_____	8. yards	_____	15. miles	_____
2. gallons	_____	9. kilograms	_____	16. feet	_____
3. inches	_____	10. cups	_____	17. ounces (oz.)	_____
4. centimeters	_____	11. meters	_____	18. liters	_____
5. millimeters	_____	12. pints	_____	19. milligrams	_____
6. pounds (lb.)	_____	13. tons	_____		
7. quarts	_____	14. kilometers (km)	_____		

Match the metric unit to a familiar amount.

20. 100 kilometers	_____	A. about 1 yard
21. 1 liter	_____	B. about a teaspoon
22. 5 grams	_____	C. the thickness of a dime
23. 25°C	_____	D. a little more than 2 pounds
24. 1 meter	_____	E. the width of a thumbtack
25. a kilogram	_____	F. about 60 miles
26. 1 millimeter	_____	G. about the weight of a new pencil
27. 1 centimeter	_____	H. about 1 pound
28. 400 grams	_____	I. the temperature of a summer day
29. 5 milliliters	_____	J. about a quart

Lesson 37

Converting among standard measurements

Volume

1 Gallon (gal.) = 4 Quarts (qt.)
1 Quart   = 2 Pints (pt.)
1 Pint   = 2 Cups (c.)

Time

1 Week = 7 Days
1 Day   = 24 Hours (hr.)
1 Hour = 60 Minutes (min.)
1 Minute = 60 Seconds (sec.)

Length

1 Mile (mi.) = 1760 Yards (yd.)
1 Mile   = 5280 Feet (ft.)
1 Yard   = 3 Feet
1 Yard   = 36 Inches (in.)
1 Foot   = 12 Inches

Weight

1 Ton (T.) = 2000 Pounds (lb.)
1 Pound   = 16 Ounces (oz.)

Rules:
1. **Multiply** to change a larger measure to a smaller measure.
2. **Divide** to change a smaller measure to a larger measure.

A.

3 yards = _____ inches

$$3 \times 36 = 108$$

B.

$1\frac{1}{2}$ feet = _____ inches

$$1\frac{1}{2} \times 12 = \frac{3}{2} \times 12 = 18$$

C.

570 seconds = _____ minutes

$$\begin{array}{r} 9\frac{1}{2} \\ 60\overline{)570} \\ \underline{540} \\ 30 \end{array}$$

Convert the measurements.

1. How many quarts are in $7\frac{1}{4}$ gallons?

_____

2. 72 hours are how many days?

_____

3. How many pounds are in 17 tons?

_____

4. 10,800 seconds are how many minutes?

_____

5. $4\frac{1}{3}$ yards are how many inches?

_____

6. $3\frac{1}{4}$ pounds are how many ounces?

_____

Objective/Convert among standard measurements.

0   5   6

Lesson 38
Working with standard measurements

Often a measurement is given in two units, for example, "a rope 1 yard 2 feet long." It is easiest to change it to a fraction of the larger unit of measure, and then solve the problem.

A.
Write 4 ounces as a fraction of a pound.

$$16 \text{ ounces} = 1 \text{ pound}$$

$$\text{or } 1 \text{ ounce} = \tfrac{1}{16} \text{ pound}$$

$$\text{So, } 4 \text{ ounces} = \tfrac{4}{16} \text{ pound} = \tfrac{1}{4} \text{ pound}$$

B.
Write 2 days 8 hours as a mixed number.

1. Write 2 days as the whole number 2.
2. Write the hours as a fraction of a day.

$$1 \text{ hour} = \tfrac{1}{24} \text{ day}$$

$$8 \text{ hours} = \tfrac{8}{24} \text{ day} = \tfrac{1}{3} \text{ day}$$

$$2 \text{ days } 8 \text{ hours is } 2\tfrac{1}{3} \text{ days.}$$

C.
Add 3 lb. 4 oz. to 4 lb. 12 oz.

$$3\tfrac{4}{16} + 4\tfrac{12}{16} = 7\tfrac{16}{16} = 8 \text{ lb.}$$

D.
Subtract 3 hr. 30 min. from 8 hr.

$$8 - 3\tfrac{1}{2} = 7\tfrac{2}{2} - 3\tfrac{1}{2} = 4\tfrac{1}{2} \text{ hr.}$$

E.
Multiply 4 ft. 9 in. by 6.

$$4\tfrac{9}{12} \times \tfrac{6}{1} = \tfrac{57}{12} \times \tfrac{6}{1} = \tfrac{57}{2} = 28\tfrac{1}{2} \text{ ft.}$$

F.
Divide 4 gal. 2 qt. by 2.

$$4\tfrac{2}{4} \div \tfrac{2}{1} = \tfrac{18}{4} \times \tfrac{1}{2} = \tfrac{9}{4} = 2\tfrac{1}{4} \text{ gal.}$$

Write the following measurements as fractions or mixed numbers.
Reduce all answers.

1. 3 quarts is what fraction of a gallon?

   _____

2. Write 2 feet 11 inches as a mixed fraction.

   _____

3. 100 pounds is what part of a ton?

   _____

4. Write 3 yards 18 inches as a mixed number.

———————

5. 50 seconds is what fraction of a minute?

———————

6. Write 12 miles 1320 feet as a mixed number.

———————

7. 12 ounces is what part of a pound?

———————

8. Write 2 hours 20 minutes as a mixed number.

———————

9. Write 5 pounds 4 ounces as a mixed number.

———————

10. 4 inches is what part of a foot?

———————

Solve the following measurement problems by first changing the measures to fractions. Then add, subtract, multiply, or divide the fractions. Reduce all answers to lowest terms.

11. 2 mi. 880 yd. ÷ 5

———————

12. 4 lb. 6 oz. × 4

———————

13. 2 yd. 2 ft. + 6 yd. 2 ft.

———————

14. 1 hr. 45 min. ÷ 7

———————

15. 3 hr. 20 min. × 3

———————

16. 4 min. 35 sec. − 50 sec.

———————

17. 2 ft. 4 in. ÷ 7

———————

18. 1 week 4 days × 5

———————

19. 6 min. 30 sec. − 5 min. 40 sec.

———————

20. 2 qt. 1 pt. + 1 pt.

———————

21. 10 yd. 2 ft. ÷ 8

———————

22. 2 miles − 2640 ft.

———————

23. 2 days 6 hr. + 7 days 12 hr.

———————

24. 5 T. 1587 lb. × 8

———————

Objective/Solve standard measurement problems.

25. A package weighs 6 pounds 2 ounces. The gift itself weighs 5 pounds 4 ounces. What is the weight of the packing materials?

_____

26. Sargon's Quarry must deliver 2 tons 300 pounds of gravel to one building site and 1700 pounds to another. What is the total amount of gravel to be delivered?

_____

27. The container for windshield-washer fluid in Fred's car holds 1 pint and 1 cup. The container must be filled 4 times a year. How much is a year's supply of fluid?

_____

28. Three people volunteered to work at the blood drive. Each one worked at the booth for 2 hours and 30 minutes. If they worked one after another, how many hours was the booth open?

_____

29. Lori Giles uses 4 gallons 3 quarts of insect spray every time she dusts her crops. Since she sprays 5 times a year, how much insect spray will she need?

_____

30. It is 20 miles from the bridge to the cabin. One mile 2640 feet of this is a gravel road. The rest is tarred. How long is the tarred road?

_____

31. Jafar bought 4 quarts of oil. He used 1 pint in the lawn mower and planned to use the rest for his car. How much did he have left for his car?

_____

For extra practice see pages 154 and 155.

Life skill
Rehabilitating a house

"This house is sound," said Annie. "Even though it looks run-down, I know we can fix it up. The whole community is working together to make this neighborhood a good place to live."

"Well, the first thing we have to work on is the kitchen," said Lew. "There are walls that need replacing and rewiring jobs to do."

1. "It's 48 feet 9 inches around the room. We need matching baseboard and ceiling molding, so we'll need a total of ____ feet."

2. "Don't forget the two doors to the kitchen. They are each 2 feet 6 inches wide, so we only need ____ feet of molding," said Annie.

3. "The outside kitchen door needs weather stripping. It's 2 feet 6 inches wide and $7\frac{1}{2}$ feet high. We'll need ____ feet of stripping to go around," Lew calculated.

4. "We should replace the rain gutters," said Lew. "The north side of the roof needs 40 feet of gutters. The south side is interrupted by the dormer windows, so we'll need $6\frac{1}{4}$ feet of gutter to the first one. Then we need $15\frac{1}{2}$ feet between them, and $6\frac{1}{4}$ feet to the end of the roof. That's a total of ____ feet of gutters."

5. "My sister said we could have that oak board for shelves," said Annie. "It's 12 feet 8 inches long. If we cut it into three shelves, that would make each shelf ____ feet long."

6. "The kitchen is 13 feet long. If the cabinets come out 2 feet 4 inches from the walls at each end, then there are ____ feet left in the length of the room," said Lew.

7. "The stove is 31 inches wide," said Annie. "We've left a space one yard wide. If we put the stove exactly in the middle, it will leave ____ inches on each side."

Life skill
Reading a time card

8:29 A.M. — 5:00 P.M.

A.M. means the hours between midnight and noon.
P.M. means the hours between noon and midnight.
The numbers on the left side of the colon (:) represent the hour.
The numbers on the right side represent the minutes past the hour.

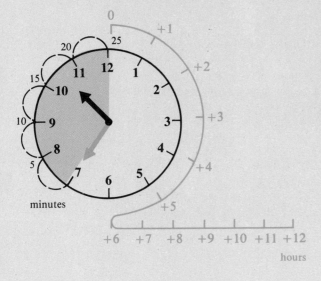

Use the clock like a number line.

Georgio Abruz worked overtime on Tuesday. He started at 10:35 A.M. and ended at 10:00 P.M. How long did he work?

He worked 25 minutes from 10:35 A.M. to 11:00 A.M. He worked 11 hours from 11:00 A.M. to 10:00 P.M.

Altogether, he worked 11 hours 25 minutes.

Figure the hours worked on these time cards.

August 17 — Garden Restaurant

		Arrived	Departed	Total hours
1.	Tim Marks	7:45 P.M.	10:45 P.M.	_____
2.	Mary Boudreau	10:15 A.M.	2:45 P.M.	_____
3.	Rick Wu	5:00 P.M.	11:40 P.M.	_____
4.	Courtney Cally	6:40 A.M.	2:10 P.M.	_____
5.	Kelly Adamis	3:30 P.M.	7:50 P.M.	_____
6.	José Hernandez	9:30 A.M.	6:00 P.M.	_____

For extra practice see page 156.

Objective/Read a time card.

Life skill
Scheduling workers

Mr. and Mrs. Bhaloo have opened a restaurant. Now they are trying to schedule their employees' work hours.

1. "We need waiters and waitresses to work from 10:30 A.M. to 11:00 P.M. That's ____ hours a day," said Mrs. Bhaloo.

   _____

2. "If we have two shifts, that means each person would work ____ hours per day."

   _____

3. "If they work 6 days a week, that's a total of ____ hours a week."

   _____

4. "We'll need someone to clear tables and carry trays and dinners," said Mr. Bhaloo. "That person should work from 11:30 A.M. to 2:30 P.M. and from 5:00 P.M. to 11:00 P.M. That's a total of ____ hours a day."

   _____

5. "And ____ hours a week Tuesday through Sunday," said Mrs. Bhaloo.

   _____

6. "We open at 11:30 A.M., but the cook will have to be here at least $1\frac{1}{2}$ hours earlier. So, that person will have to arrive by ____."

   _____

7. "We close at 11:00 P.M., but we need 2 people to clean. They'll have to stay an extra 45 minutes to finish. So, they'll get off at ____," finished Mrs. Bhaloo.

   _____

8. "We will serve meals from 11:30 A.M. to 10:00 P.M., 6 days a week. That's a total of ____ hours a week," Mr. Bhaloo said, putting down his pencil.

   _____

Lesson 39
Calculating the unit price

To comparison shop, you must compare prices for the same unit of measure.

A.

Which is the better buy, cider at $1.52 a gallon or at $.40 a quart? Assume the quality is equal.

$$\frac{\text{price}}{\text{unit}}: \quad \frac{\$1.52}{\text{gallon}} \quad \textbf{or} \quad \frac{\$.40}{\text{quart}}$$

1. Choose a working unit.   The working unit is 1 quart.   1 gal. = 4 qt.

2. Change bottom measures to the working unit.

$$\frac{\$1.52}{4 \text{ qt.}} \quad \textbf{or} \quad \frac{\$.40}{\text{qt.}}$$

3. Change the price ratio to price per 1 unit.

$$\begin{array}{r} .38 \\ 4\overline{)1.52} \\ \underline{1\ 2} \\ 32 \end{array} \rightarrow \frac{\$.38}{\text{qt.}} \quad \textbf{or} \quad \frac{\$.40}{\text{qt.}}$$

The gallon of cider is the better buy.

B.

Which is the better buy, pre-packaged lunch meat at 99¢ for 10 ounces, or lunch meat cut from a bulk piece at $1.39 a pound?

$$\frac{\text{price}}{\text{unit}}: \quad \frac{\$1.39}{\text{lb.}} \quad \textbf{or} \quad \frac{\$.99}{10 \text{ oz.}}$$

1. The working unit can be the ounce.   16 oz. = 1 lb.

2. $\dfrac{\$1.39}{16 \text{ oz.}}$ **or** $\dfrac{\$.99}{10 \text{ oz.}}$

3.

$$\begin{array}{r} 8\frac{11}{16}¢ \\ 16\overline{)1.39} \\ \underline{1\ 28} \\ 11 \end{array} \rightarrow \frac{8\frac{11}{16}¢}{\text{oz.}} \quad \textbf{or} \quad \frac{9\frac{9}{10}¢}{\text{oz.}} \leftarrow \begin{array}{r} 9\frac{9}{10}¢ \\ 10\overline{).99} \\ \underline{90} \\ 9 \end{array}$$

The lunch meat cut from a bulk piece is cheaper.

Objective/Calculate unit price.

Fresh orange juice, $1.89 a gallon

Milk, $.99 a half gallon

Cream, 59¢ a half pint

Canned tomatoes, 28 ounces for 70¢

2 pounds of bacon for $2.96

Frozen orange juice, $1.48,
makes 3 quarts

Milk, 64¢ a quart

Cream, $1.10 a pint

Canned tomatoes, 1 lb. 8 oz. for 54¢

20 ounces of bacon for $1.95

Find the unit price for each item. Circle the best buy.

1. Orange juice, _____ a quart

2. Orange juice, _____ a quart

3. Milk, _____ a quart

4. Milk, _____ a quart

5. Cream, _____ a cup

6. Cream, _____ a cup

7. Canned tomatoes, _____ an ounce

8. Canned tomatoes, _____ an ounce

9. Bacon, _____ a pound

10. Bacon, _____ a pound

For extra practice see page 157.

Objective/Calculate unit price.

Lesson 40
Reading a thermometer

A thermometer measures temperature in degrees. The symbol for degree is °.

The two most common scales for measuring temperature are the Celsius and Fahrenheit scales. People living in countries using the metric system and scientists everywhere use the Celsius scale. Most people in the United States use the Fahrenheit scale.

Many thermometers have both scales drawn on them. It is important to show which size degrees you are using.

Write °F for degrees Fahrenheit. Write °C for degrees Celsius.

Look at the diagram of a thermometer. What is the normal body temperature?

37°C or 98.6°F

The temperature is written two ways, but both ways indicate the **same** warmth.

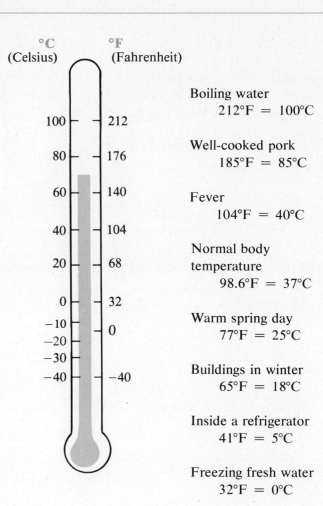

°C
(Celsius)

°F
(Fahrenheit)

Boiling water
212°F = 100°C

Well-cooked pork
185°F = 85°C

Fever
104°F = 40°C

Normal body temperature
98.6°F = 37°C

Warm spring day
77°F = 25°C

Buildings in winter
65°F = 18°C

Inside a refrigerator
41°F = 5°C

Freezing fresh water
32°F = 0°C

Freezing ocean water
25.6°F = −3.4°C

Use the diagram to answer these questions.

1. A person with a fever might have a temperature of _____ °F or _____ °C

2. Fresh water freezes at _____ °F or _____ °C

3. Businesses are supposed to heat buildings to _____ °F or _____ °C

4. Water boils at _____ °F or _____ °C

5. The inside of a refrigerator is about _____ °F or _____ °C

6. A warm spring day might have a temperature of about _____ °F or _____ °C

Objective/Read and compare temperature scales.

0   5   6

Lesson 41
Converting among metric measurements

The metric measurement system is used all over the world. It is simple to use, since it is based on the decimal system. If you know how adding prefixes to the base unit changes the value of the measurement, you can use the metric system.

Base units   **Gram** (g) means weight, about three aspirins.
Liter (*l*) means volume, about a quart.
Meter (m) means length, about one yard.

Prefixes   **Kilo** means 1000 base units.

1 kilogram	= 1000 grams	or 1 g = .001 kg
1 kiloliter	= 1000 liters	1 *l* = .001 k*l*
1 kilometer	= 1000 meters	1 m = .001 km

Milli means .001 base unit.

1 milligram	= .001 gram	or 1 g = 1000 mg
1 milliliter	= .001 liter	1 *l* = 1000 m*l*
1 millimeter	= .001 meter	1 m = 1000 mm

Centi means .01 base unit. It is only used with length measurements.
    1 centimeter = .01 meter   or 1 cm = .01 m

A.
$$48 \text{ kg} = \underline{\hspace{1cm}} \text{ g}$$
$$48 \text{ kg} \times \frac{1000 \text{ g}}{\text{kg}} = 48{,}000 \text{ g}$$

B.
$$53 \text{ m}l = \underline{\hspace{1cm}} l$$
$$53 \text{ m}l \times \frac{.001 \text{ } l}{\text{m}l} = .053 \text{ } l$$

C.
$$5963 \text{ m} = \underline{\hspace{1cm}} \text{ km}$$
$$5963 \text{ m} \times \frac{.001 \text{ km}}{\text{m}} = 5.963 \text{ km}$$

Convert each measurement into the other units across the line.

Kilo	Base	Centi	Milli
37 km	1. _____ m	2. _____ cm	3. _____ mm
4. _____ kg	142 g		5. _____ mg
6. _____ km	7. _____ m	5 cm	8. _____ mm
34,005 kg	9. _____ g		10. _____ mg
11. _____ k*l*	27 *l*		12. _____ m*l*

Lesson 42
Working with metric measurements

In order to work with metric measurements, change two-unit measurements into decimal values of the larger unit.

A.
Write 4 km 578 m as a decimal.

1. Write 4 km as a whole number.
2. Change 578 m to km by multiplying by .001.

$$
\begin{array}{r}
4.000 \text{ km} \\
+ \ .578 \text{ km} \\
\hline
4.578 \text{ km}
\end{array}
$$

B.
Write 2 *l* 51 m*l* as a decimal.

1. Write 2 *l* as a whole number.
2. Change 51 m*l* to liters by multiplying by .001.

$$
\begin{array}{r}
2.000 \ l \\
+ \ .051 \ l \\
\hline
2.051 \ l
\end{array}
$$

C.
Add. 1 m 95 cm + 5 cm
Write the measures as decimals.

$$
\begin{array}{r}
1.95 \text{ m} \\
+ \ .05 \text{ m} \\
\hline
2.00 \text{ m}
\end{array}
$$

D.
Divide. 12 kg 44 g ÷ 4

$$
\begin{array}{r}
3.011 \text{ kg} \\
4\overline{)12.044} \text{ kg}
\end{array}
$$

Change these to single-unit measurements.

1. 5 *l* 692 m*l* _____
2. 79 m 52 mm _____
3. 46 km 56 m _____

4. 9 km 798 m _____
5. 6 k*l* 25 *l* _____
6. 78 m 45 cm _____

7. 22 g 992 mg _____
8. 59 kg 26 g _____
9. 11 *l* 546 m*l* _____

Solve.

10. 50 k*l* 450 *l* × 6.5 _____
11. 3 m 20 cm ÷ 12 _____
12. 3 *l* 5 m*l* × 47 _____

13. 9.3 m*l* × 5 _____
14. 6 *l* 756 m*l* ÷ 4 _____
15. 92 kg + 66 mg _____

16.
$$
\begin{array}{r}
7 \text{ kg } 600 \text{ g} \\
+ \ 14 \text{ kg } 900 \text{ g} \\
\hline
\end{array}
$$

17.
$$
\begin{array}{r}
1 \ l \ 200 \text{ m}l \\
- \ \ \ \ \ 800 \text{ m}l \\
\hline
\end{array}
$$

18.
$$
\begin{array}{r}
10 \text{ km } 200 \text{ m} \\
- \ 7 \text{ km } 500 \text{ m} \\
\hline
\end{array}
$$

19.
$$
\begin{array}{r}
2 \text{ g } \ \ 55 \text{ mg} \\
+ \ 1 \text{ g } 788 \text{ mg} \\
\hline
\end{array}
$$

Objective/Work with metric measurements.

Solve each problem. Fill in the space under the letter of the correct answer.

20. To make a punch for 30 people, Salvador needs 4 l 250 ml of ginger ale and 5 l 800 ml of fruit drink. What volume will that make?

    a. 9 l   c. 1.55 l
    b. 10.05 l   d. 10 l

a	b	c	d
||	||	||	||

21. J.J.'s Market bought 7 kg 200 g of grapes and sold 5 kg 850 g. What remained at the end of the day?

    a. 12 kg   c. 13 kg
    b. 1.35 kg   d. 1 kg 150 g

a	b	c	d
||	||	||	||

22. Trim for one side of the shed takes 3 m 30 cm. How much trim will be needed for all four sides?

    a. 12 m   c. 13.2 cm
    b. 13.2 m   d. 7.3 m

a	b	c	d
||	||	||	||

23. 6 kg 400 g of apples were to be divided among 8 containers. What was the total weight of each container if an empty container weighed 500 g?

    a. 1 kg   c. .8 kg
    b. 1.3 kg   d. 2.1 kg

a	b	c	d
||	||	||	||

24. Mary made 1 liter of photographic developer. She used 250 ml to develop 3 rolls of film. How much was left over?

    a. .75 l   c. 7.5 l
    b. .250 l   d. 75 l

a	b	c	d
||	||	||	||

25. 5 l 500 ml of juice was brought to serve the 22 blood donors when they were finished. What was the amount of each serving?

    a. 250 ml   c. 100 ml
    b. .25 ml   d. 2.5 l

a	b	c	d
||	||	||	||

26. 4 m 40 cm of 80-cm-wide plastic sheet was used to cover 4 windows. What was the average amount used on each window?

    a. 9 cm   c. 33 cm
    b. 1.1 m   d. 17.6 m

a	b	c	d
||	||	||	||

For extra practice see pages 158 and 159.

0   21   26

Objective/Work with metric measurements.

"Our apartment needs some work before winter. Don't forget the lease we signed says we pay for heat," said Diana.

"You're right," said Thaddeus. "If we weatherize it now, we'll save some money on heating bills."

1. "We have 3 large windows. The distance around each one is 6 m 25 cm. We'll need _____ meters of weather stripping for them."

            _____

2. "We'll need 6 meters 75 centimeters of stripping for the door. That's a total of _____ meters of weather stripping."

            _____

3. "At 40¢ a meter, that will cost _____."

            _____

4. "If we buy clear plastic to cover the windows we will cut down on heat loss. The plastic is wide enough to cover the width, so we only need 6 meters to cover the length. Add 16 cm for each of the 3 windows for overlap. That's a total of _____ m of plastic."

            _____

5. "At $2.50 a meter, that's $_____. It seems expensive, but if we're careful we can use it for more than one year."

            _____

6. "350 grams of caulking compound will cover about 30 meters. I think we're going to need to cover about 3 times that much. So we'd better get _____ gm of caulk."

            _____

Life skill
Comparing costs of generic and brand-name medicines

Rules:
1. Assume the quality is equal.

2. Find the cost per unit of each product.

3. Compare the cost of the generic medicine with the cost of the brand-name medicine.

4. Circle the product that is the better buy.

Vocabulary:

Generic means no-brand packaging.

Brand name means a well-known product.

Generic

aspirin, 200 tablets, 5 g each	$2.25
cold pills, 25 g, 100 tablets	3.50
cough syrup, 300 ml	2.91
vitamins, 150 g	3.00

Brand Name

Star Aspirin, 500 g bottle	$1.60
Ace Cold Pills, 50 g, 100 tablets	8.00
Super Cough Syrup, 350 ml	3.50
Peppy Vitamins, 200 g	5.00

Generic

1. aspirin, _____ per g

3. cold pills, _____ per g

5. cough syrup, _____ per ml

7. vitamins, _____ per g

Brand Name

2. Star Aspirin, _____ per g

4. Ace Cold Pills, _____ per g

6. Super Cough Syrup, _____ per ml

8. Peppy Vitamins, _____ per g

Objective/Calculate and compare unit prices.

Figuring meal portions

"I really like working here in the cafeteria," said Frances. "The new responsibility of getting the food out on trays is exciting. Doing it all in metrics makes it easier."

1. "I have 10 liters of orange juice for 40 trays. So each patient will get _____ milliliters."

   _____

2. "40 patients ordered chopped steak. Each steak weighs 125 g. I'll need _____ kilograms of cooked, chopped steak for dinner."

   _____

3. "I have 5 kilograms of cooked liver. Since each serving must be 200 grams, I can serve _____ patients."

   _____

4. "I have 145 orders for potatoes at 200 grams a serving. I'll need _____ kilograms of potatoes tonight."

   _____

5. "I've made 44 liters of soup. That will serve 160 people, with each person getting _____ ml per bowl."

   _____

6. "65 people asked for veal steak. Each piece weighs 72 grams. Each plate gets 2 pieces, so I'll need _____ kilograms of veal."

   _____

7. "It's mixed vegetables tonight. 8 kg 500 g of carrots, 5 kg 600 g of peas, 6 kg of wax beans, and 7 kg 200 g of lima beans will make a total of _____ kg of vegetables."

   _____

8. "If each person gets 175 grams of vegetables, I can serve _____ people."

   _____

Posttest/Unit 8

1. Mike must make deliveries by truck. First, he'll drive 4 km 587 m to Bremerton; from there he'll drive 12 km 754 m to Hanover and 8 km 784 m back to the shop. How far will he drive? _____

2. The Morningside Bakery had 16 pounds 1 ounce of flour for bread. After making 10 loaves, they had 4 lb. 5 oz. left. How much did they use? _____

3. The boss wanted 5 similar projects finished in 2 hours and 30 minutes. How much time should Felix spend on each one? _____

4. Carrie plans to fill 8 canning jars with tomato sauce. Each one holds 1 liter 237 m*l* of sauce. How much should she prepare? _____

5. Bill bought boards 4 feet 2 inches in length to make a bookcase. When he got home, he realized they were 8 inches too long. How long should the boards have been? _____

6. The blood drive collected 950 m*l* of blood from every donor. If 55 people gave, how many liters of blood did the drive collect that day? _____

7. Serena is in charge of keeping all the machines in the factory oiled. If she uses 5*l* 15 m*l* of oil a day, how much will she use at the end of 365 days? _____

8. Ilia wanted to make 4 times a recipe which called for 900 grams of berries. How many kilograms of berries does he need altogether? _____

AAA Hardware	
3 1-liter cans of car oil	$2.10
Towing chain, 6-foot length	3.00
5 kg of charcoal	3.95
1 quart charcoal lighter	.95

BBB Home Improvement Center	
1 150-m*l* can of car oil	$1.20
towing chain	.45/ft.
charcoal	.80/kg
charcoal lighter	.45/pint

Find the cost per unit. Then circle the better buy.

AAA

9. car oil, _____ per m*l*

BBB

10. car oil, _____ per m*l*

11. towing chain, _____ per ft.

12. towing chain, _____ per ft.

13. charcoal, _____ per kg

14. charcoal, _____ per kg

15. charcoal lighter, _____ per pint

16. charcoal lighter, _____ per pint

Proportion, graphs, and measurement

Solve.

1. "This car costs 25¢ a mile to drive. So far we've driven 900 miles. That is a total cost of $_____." _____

2. "We've used 36 gallons of gas so far. That means we're getting _____ miles to the gallon." _____

3. "That 900 miles is only 20 inches on the map. That means each inch stands for _____ miles." _____

4. "We drove that distance in 18 hours. That's an average of _____ miles an hour." _____

5. "The map shows we have 3 more inches to go. That's only _____ miles." _____

6. "If we make 45 miles an hour, we'll be there in _____ hours." _____

7. "For every 20 miles, we paid 40¢ in tolls. We've driven 900 miles, so we've spent $_____ on tolls." _____

8. The PTA planned a chili dinner to make money for the school. They made 5 gallons 2 quarts of punch and used 4 gallons 3 quarts. How much was left over?

      _____

9. They cooked 10 pounds 9 ounces of meat in one pan and 13 pounds 6 ounces in the other. How much meat did they cook in all?

      _____

10. They bought 5 large-sized cans of tomatoes. Each weighed 2 kilograms 250 grams. How many kilograms did they buy?

      _____

11. They needed to set up tables for large groups. To do that, they put 2 tables end-to-end. Each table was 2 meters 250 millimeters long. How long were the two tables together?

      _____

12. Eight PTA volunteers worked 2 hours and 15 minutes each. What was the total number of hours worked by all the volunteers?

      _____

A Town Market	*B* Super Mart
1 lb. 2 oz. pkg. of frozen peas, $1.70	36 oz. pkg. of frozen peas, $1.62
500 grams of hamburger, $1.45	1 kilogram of hamburger, $2.85
750 m*l* of orange juice, $1.35	1 liter of orange juice, $1.50
2 quarts of milk, $.98	1 gallon of milk, $1.89

Write the letter *A* or *B* to show which store has the better buy.

13. peas   **14.** hamburger   **15.** juice   **16.** milk

_____   _____   _____   _____

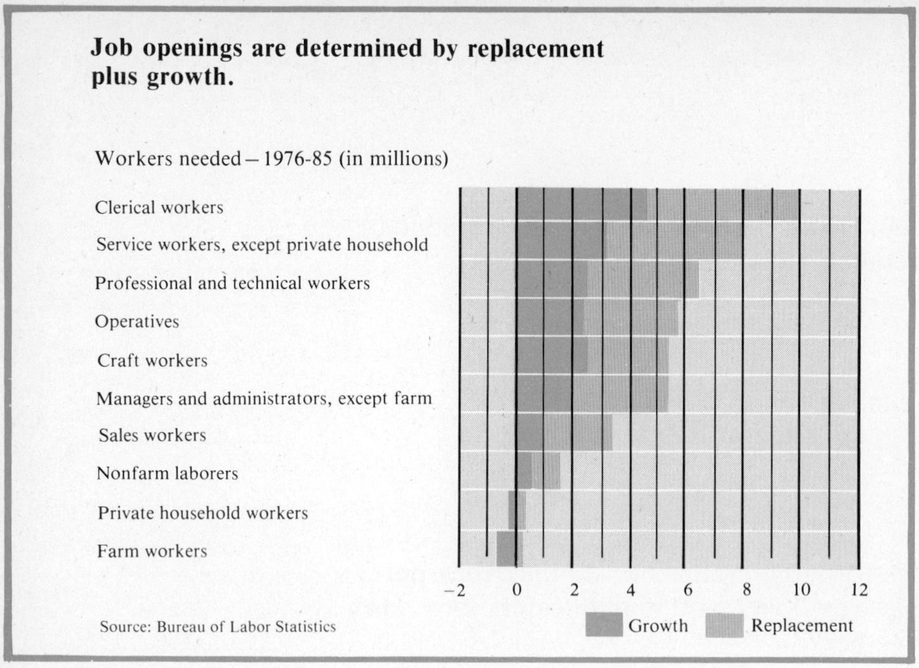
Job openings are determined by replacement plus growth.
Workers needed – 1976-85 (in millions)
Clerical workers
Service workers, except private household
Professional and technical workers
Operatives
Craft workers
Managers and administrators, except farm
Sales workers
Nonfarm laborers
Private household workers
Farm workers
−2
0
2
4
6
8
10
12
Source: Bureau of Labor Statistics
Growth
Replacement

17. Which group of jobs will have the largest number of openings? ________________

18. About how many openings will that be? ________________

19. Which group of jobs will have the least number of openings? ________________

20. About how many openings will that be? ________________

21. What is the difference in the number of openings between service jobs and sales jobs? ________________

22. What is the approximate ratio of salespeople to managers? ________________

23. How many more new jobs will there be for clerical workers than for service workers? ________________

Work through the Life skill lesson on preparing your income tax return on pages 160–162 and the Sample pre-employment test on pages 163 and 164.

KEY/Lesson 29 1–7 Lesson 38 8, 9, 12 Lesson 42 10, 11
Lesson 33 17–23 Lesson 39 13–16

Part 2 test

1. Mike Wyzinski must drive around the city to get orders for the machine parts he sells. Last week he drove a total of 324 miles. His company gives him $.17 a mile to cover the cost of using his car. What will he receive for last week's mileage allowance?   _____

2. In order to drive that distance, he needed 20 gallons of gasoline. How many miles does his car get to the gallon?   _____

3. He receives a $50 commission for every $1000 of machine parts he sells. He earned $225 in commissions that week. What was his sales total?   _____

4. Mike usually makes one sale for every three customers he contacts. He contacted 42 customers last week. How many sales did he make?   _____

5. Mike spends 7 hours on the road for each hour he spends at the company plant. Write that as a ratio.   _____

6. A customer is located $2\frac{5}{8}$ inch away from the company plant on Mike's map. The map scale is 12 miles to the inch. How many miles will Mike drive to deliver the customer's order?   _____

7. Drill bits are ordered in packages of 24. Each package costs $72.00. What is the cost of 17 drill bits?   _____

8. The Randalls had a house-painting party. They had 5 gallons of paint and used 4 gallons and 1 quart. How much paint did they have left over?

_____

9. All eight of them worked 4 hours and 15 minutes each. What was the total number of hours they spent painting?

_____

10. Halli and Oscar painted the baseboard trim a dark brown. There were 36 feet of trim for the den, 20 feet 8 inches for the hall, 52 feet 4 inches for the living room, and 48 feet 8 inches for the dining room. How many feet of trim were there in all?

_____

11. They had hamburgers for lunch. One kilogram 448 grams of meat made 12 hamburgers. What did each hamburger weigh?

_____

12. They served 750 grams of potato salad. It made 8 servings. What did each serving weigh?

_____

A Sawyer's Market

Whole fryer chicken, $2\frac{1}{4}$ lb. average	$1.35
Sour cream, 1 cup	.60
Potatoes, $5\frac{1}{2}$-kilogram sack	1.10
Vinegar, 1-liter bottle	.35

B Nick's Finer Foods

Fryer chicken, 56¢ per pound
Sour cream, $1.10 per pint
Potatoes, 22¢ per kilogram
Vinegar, $1\frac{1}{4}$ liters for 40¢

Write *A* or *B* to show which store has the better buy.

13. chicken   _____

14. sour cream   _____

15. potatoes   _____

16. vinegar   _____

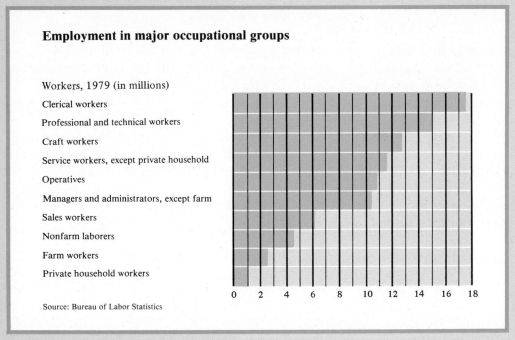

Employment in major occupational groups

Workers, 1979 (in millions)
Clerical workers
Professional and technical workers
Craft workers
Service workers, except private household
Operatives
Managers and administrators, except farm
Sales workers
Nonfarm laborers
Farm workers
Private household workers

0 2 4 6 8 10 12 14 16 18

Source: Bureau of Labor Statistics

17. What is the largest group of workers? _____

18. Approximately how many people work at that job? _____

19. What is the smallest group of workers? _____

20. Approximately how many people work at that job? _____

21. What is the ratio between craft workers and nonfarm laborers? _____

22. What is the difference between the number of farm workers and the number of clerical workers? _____

23. How many more people work at the professions than at crafts? _____

Understanding word problems

Recognizing clue words

Every word problem has clues to help you solve it. Here is a list of clue words. Watch for them in problems. They will help you decide when to add, subtract, divide, or multiply.

Addition clues
-er endings, like wider, higher, longer; increase; mark-up; more; plus; sum; total

Subtraction clues
-er endings, like smaller, lower, shorter, fewer; discount; difference; deduct; left over; less than; off; reduced by; remainder; mark down

Multiplication clues
product, times, at (6 cans at 12¢ a can), of ($\frac{1}{2}$ of 18, or .5 of 18, or 50% of 18)

Division clues
divide, quotient, share equally, per, how many ____ in ____?

Clues to multiplication or addition
total, altogether, in all

Working with terms

Average
Find the total of the group of numbers. Divide by the number of numbers that made the total.

Three days of shrimp trawling netted the following: $\frac{1}{3}$ ton, $\frac{1}{2}$ ton, and $\frac{1}{6}$ ton of shrimp. What was the average daily catch?

$$\frac{(\frac{1}{3} + \frac{1}{2} + \frac{1}{6}) \text{ ton}}{3 \text{ days}} = \frac{\frac{1}{3} \text{ ton}}{\text{day}}$$

Interest
Interest = principal $\times$ rate $\times$ time.

Percent

% of whole — Multiply the part by 100. Divide the answer by the whole.

part amount — Multiply the whole by the percent. Divide the answer by 100.

whole amount — Multiply the part by 100. Divide the answer by the percent.

Proportion
Use a proportion when a problem gives a ratio between two quantities, A and B. Ask, if A is changed, how should B change?

6 apple trees yield 15 bushels of fruit. How many bushels will 10 trees yield?
$$\frac{15}{6} = \frac{n}{10}$$

Word list

Budget   Planned spending of money. p. 41

Centi   Metric prefix, .01 of the base unit. p. 119

Commission   Income based on a fixed % of total sales. p. 44

Consumer price index   Measure of the changing value of a dollar. p. 98

Down payment   Part of total cost to be paid at once, as part of an installment plan. pp. 32, 54

Estimate   A guess based on good reasons. p. 35

Finance charge   Interest on installment plan loan. p. 54

Gram   Metric base unit for weight. pp. 104, 119

Horizontal   The direction across the page. p. 94

Installment plan   Payment stretched over time, requiring a down payment and monthly payments with a finance charge. p. 54

Interest   Cost of borrowing money. p. 47

Intersect   To cross, as a row crosses a column. p. 96

Key   A chart of symbols and what they mean. p. 90

Kilo   Metric prefix, 1000 times the base unit. p. 119

Liter   Metric base unit for volume. pp. 104, 119

Meter   Metric base unit for length. pp. 104, 119

Milli   Metric prefix, .001 of the base unit. p. 119

Overhead   Cost of running a business. p. 44

Percent   A ratio of a part to a whole which has been divided into 100 equal parts. p. 15

Principal   Amount of a loan. p. 47

Projection   An estimate of future change. p. 94

Proportion   2 equal ratios. p. 73

Rate   The cost per year of borrowing money; for example, 10% of the principal per year. p. 47

Ratio   The relationship between two numbers. p. 71

Sales tax   % of bill of sale that supports government. pp. 29, 32, 44

Symbol   A picture that stands for something. p. 90

Vertical   The direction down the page. p. 94

Life skill/Saving energy

There are many ways to save energy. Oil companies, electric companies, and aluminum companies are among those who tell us how to conserve.

Solve the following problems. Decide how you can save energy.

1. A car gets 20% better mileage when it is driven at 55 m.p.h. instead of 65 m.p.h. If you drove 100 miles at 65 m.p.h., how much farther could you have driven at 55 m.p.h.?

   _____

2. By getting a tune-up and properly inflating the tires on his car, Ed Trawinski improved his gasoline mileage by 10%. If he drove 100 miles on six gallons of gas before, how many more miles can he drive on the same amount now?

   _____

3. One make of car gets 50% better mileage on the highway than in the city. How much farther than 100 miles can it go if it is driven on the highway instead of in the city?

   _____

4. Recycling aluminum cans saves 95% of the energy needed to make new aluminum cans from ore. If it takes 100 units of energy to make one aluminum can from ore, how many units of energy can be saved by using recycled aluminum?

   _____

5. A fluorescent tube can provide the same amount of light as a regular light bulb while using only $16\frac{2}{3}\%$ of the electricity. If the regular light bulb uses 100 watts of electricity, how many watts does the fluorescent tube use to give the same amount of light?

   _____

6. In A.D. 2000 the United States will need 200% more electricity than it uses today. For every 100 units of electricity the nation uses now, how many units will be needed in the year 2000?

   _____

USE WITH Lesson 11   What percents mean

Practice/Writing equal fractions, decimals, and percents

Fill in the chart by changing the given fraction, decimal, or percent to the other forms.

	Fraction	Percent	Decimal
1.	_____	50%	_____
2.	_____	_____	.33 $\frac{1}{3}$
3.	$\frac{1}{10}$	_____	_____
4.	_____	_____	1.35
5.	_____	16 $\frac{2}{3}$%	_____
6.	$\frac{5}{8}$	_____	_____
7.	_____	_____	.005
8.	$\frac{1}{500}$	_____	_____
9.	_____	1 $\frac{1}{2}$% or 1.5%	_____
10.	$\frac{99}{100}$	_____	_____
11.	_____	2557%	_____
12.	_____	_____	.90

Life skill/Comparing facts given as percents

The results of surveys and polls, as well as other facts, often are given in percents rather than actual figures. Think about the percents in the examples below. Decide whether percents are helpful or misleading.

Solve these problems.

1. A teacher said that 80% of the people he asked wanted weekly tests. Only 4 people wanted weekly tests. How many people did the teacher ask?

    _____

2. One million people voted to reelect the governor, but he lost. He got only 12.5% of the vote. How many people voted?

    _____

3. Two different toothpaste companies reported that 80% of the people they surveyed used their brands. Company A supported its claim with favorable results from 80 people. Company B supported its claim with favorable results from 1280 people. (a) How many people did Company A survey? (b) How many people did Company B survey?

    a. _____

    b. _____

4. Two car companies advertise that their new car models get 50% better mileage than last year's models. Car A got 12 miles to the gallon last year. Car B got 20 miles to the gallon last year. (a) How many miles per gallon does Car A get this year? (b) How many miles per gallon does Car B get this year?

    a. _____

    b. _____

5. In the United States, 73.5% of the people live in cities. That's 161,320,740 people. In Canada, 76.1% of the people live in cities, but that's only 17,883,500 people. (a) How many people live in the United States? (b) How many people live in Canada?

    a. _____

    b. _____

Life skill/Figuring property tax

Every home has many values.

Current market value is the price for which the home can be sold.
Replacement value is the cost of rebuilding it from scratch.
Assessed value is the value given it by a tax assessor. This is
often a percentage of the current market value.

Property tax is based on the assessed value of the home.

From the information given, find the assessed value and the property tax for each family's home. The first is worked as an example.

Current market value	Assessed value (60% of current market value)	Tax rate	Annual property tax
1. Jackson $42,000	$42,000 × .60 = $25,200	3.5%	$25,200 × .035 = $882.00
2. Hernandez $51,500	_____	3.5%	_____
3. Leong $67,200	_____	3.5%	_____
4. Martinelli $49,900	_____	2.5%	_____
5. Weinberg $55,400	_____	2.5%	_____
6. Littlebird $58,000	_____	2.75%	_____
7. McGee $70,000	_____	3.0%	_____
8. Olson $89,000	_____	2.5%	_____

Life skill/Buying at a discount

The local hardware store was having a tool sale. The Neighborhood Rehab Co-op wanted some new tools. They decided to figure out how much they would actually save on the different items. They made a list of the current prices and the other information they knew—either the dollar discount or the sale price.

Fill in the blanks with the missing information.

Item	Current price	Percent of discount	Dollar discount	Sale price
1. Hammer	$ 8.00	_____	$ 3.50	_____
2. Saw blade	$ 1.50	_____	_____	$ .75
3. Screwdriver	$ 5.00	_____	$ 1.25	_____
4. Wrench set	$20.00	_____	_____	$13.50
5. Drill	$28.80	_____	$12.96	_____
6. Electric saw	$69.90	_____	_____	$46.60
7. Workbench	$29.00	_____	$11.89	_____
8. T-squares	$ 5.10	_____	_____	$ 4.25

USE WITH Lesson 21 Solving for the percent

Practice/Solving percent problems

Solve.

1. What is 40% of 164? _____

2. 90 is 75% of what? _____

3. 44 is what percent of 132? _____

4. What is 85% of 600? _____

5. 5.5% of what is 32.01? _____

6. $1 \frac{1}{2}$ is what percent of 3? _____

7. What is 50% of .01? _____

8. 16% of what is 12? _____

9. $\frac{1}{3}$ is what percent of $\frac{2}{3}$? _____

10. What is 5% of 34? _____

11. .5% of what is .0125? _____

12. 17 is what percent of 51? _____

13. 50% of 188 is what? _____

14. 63% of what is 315? _____

15. 25 is what percent of 300? _____

16. 42% of what is 882? _____

17. What is 20% of 15? _____

18. .5 is 50% of what? _____

19. 25 is what percent of 125? _____

20. 17% of what is 952? _____

21. $12 \frac{2}{3}$ is what percent of 38? _____

22. What is 3% of 99? _____

23. 1.086 is what percent of 90.5? _____

24. 14 is what percent of 21? _____

Life skill/Interpreting voting results

Voting results are often given in percents. Complete the table below from the information given. Then answer the questions.

	Total votes	Votes for Candidate A	Percent of total	Votes for Candidate B	Percent of total
Precinct 1	6,500	2,925	_____	3,575	_____
Precinct 2	8,000	_____	51%	_____	49%
Precinct 3	7,500	_____	$33\frac{1}{3}$%	5,000	_____
Precinct 4	_____	6,975	62%	4,275	_____
Precinct 5	9,400	_____	38%	_____	62%
Precinct 6	10,250	5,125	_____	_____	50%
Grand totals	_____	_____		_____	

1. What is the total number of votes?   _____

2. What is the total number of votes for Candidate A?   _____

3. What is the total number of votes for Candidate B?   _____

4. What percent of the grand total vote is the total vote for Candidate A? (Round the answer to the nearest whole percent.)   _____

5. What percent of the grand total vote is the total vote for Candidate B? (Round the answer to the nearest whole percent.)   _____

6. Which candidate won the election?   _____

7. Is it easier to tell who's winning from the vote totals or the percents?

_____

USE WITH Lesson 22 Deciding how to solve a percent problem

Life skill/Buying a car

Doug and Niki Henderson are finally able to buy a new car. Help them figure out their monthly payments and the total cost by solving these problems.

1. "We have saved $60 a month for 2 years. It wasn't always easy, but we have a total of $_____."

    _____

2. "We can put a 20% down payment on a $6,525 car. That is $_____."

    _____

3. "We need a loan for $_____."

    _____

4. "We can get a 36-month loan. The amount of money we pay back on the loan each month will be $_____ not including interest."

    _____

5. "The interest on the loan will be 9% a year. The interest is on the complete amount of the loan. That is $_____ interest each year."

    _____

6. "We will pay a total of $_____ interest for the three years."

    _____

7. "The amount of money we pay for interest each month will be $_____."

    _____

8. "The total monthly payment to the bank will be $_____."

    _____

9. "The total amount of money we will pay to the bank for the three years will be $_____."

    _____

10. "We will have paid $_____ total for the car."

    _____

11. "That is _____% more than the price on the price sticker."

    _____

Calculators/Solving percent problems

To solve percent problems on a simple calculator like the one shown here, all percents must be changed to decimals, and decimals back into percents.

Remember: To change percents to decimals
1. Drop the % sign.
2. Move the decimal point 2 places to the left.

decimals to percents
1. Move the decimal point 2 places to the right.
2. Add the % sign.

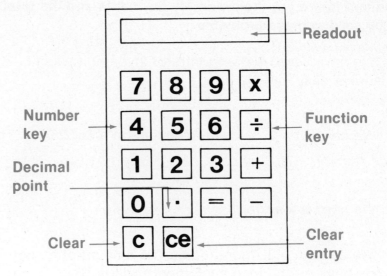

Readout

Number key

Function key

Decimal point

Clear

Clear entry

What is 15% of 48? (Solve for the part.)
Change 15% to .15.
Press ⊡ ⊡ ⑤ .
Press ⊠ .
Press ④ ⑧ .
Press ⊟ .
Read the answer and write it down.
___7.2___
Press Ⓒ before starting the next problem.

362 is 25% of what? (Solve for the whole.)
Change 25% to .25.
Press ③ ⑥ ② .
Press ÷ .
Press ⊡ ② ⑤ .
Press ⊟ .
Read the answer and write it down.
___1448___
Press Ⓒ before starting the next problem.

3.75 is what percent of 25?
(Solve for the percent.)
Press ③ ⊡ ⑦ ⑤ .
Press ÷ .
Press ② ⑤ .
Press ⊟ .
Read the answer. It is a decimal. To change the decimal to a percent, multiply by 100.
Press ⊠ .
Press ① ⓪ ⓪ .
Press ⊟ .
Write the answer. Add the % sign.
___15%___

Work these problems on a calculator.

1. 850 is 20% of what? _____

2. What is 63% of 98? _____

3. What is 152% of 420? _____

4. 7.75 is 110% of what? _____

5. 250 is what percent of 575? _____

Calculators/Finding compound interest

Interest can be figured every 3 months and added to the balance quarterly. Interest can also be figured every 6 months and added to the balance semi-annually.

Quarterly is $\frac{1}{4}$ (or .25) of a year.

Semi-annually is $\frac{1}{2}$ (or .50) of a year.

Remember to use only decimals on the calculator.

What is 5% interest on $200 figured semi-annually?

Press ② ⓪ ⓪ .
Press ✕ .
Press · ⓪ ⑤ . (for 5%)
Press ✕ .
Press · ⑤ . (for half a year)
Press = .
Add the answer to 200.
200 + 5 = $205

Press ② ⓪ ⑤ . (new balance)
Press ✕ .
Press · ⓪ ⑤ .
Press ✕ .
Press · ⑤ .
Press = .
Add this answer to 205.
205 + 5.13 = $210.13 (final balance)

**Carlos saved $1000. Fill in the following bank statements.
Circle the one that offers him the best interest rate.**

3-month savings certificate at 5 $\frac{3}{4}$% for 1 year.

		Deposit	Withdrawal	Interest	Balance
1.	1st 3 months	$1000.00		_____	_____
2.	2nd 3 months			_____	_____
3.	3rd 3 months			_____	_____
4.	4th 3 months			_____	_____
5.	Total			_____	_____

6-month savings certificate at 6 $\frac{1}{4}$% for 1 year.

		Deposit	Withdrawal	Interest	Balance
6.	1st 6 months	$1000.00		_____	_____
7.	2nd 6 months			_____	_____
8.	Total			_____	_____

Practice/Installment buying

Solve. Round the answers to the nearest whole percent.

A side of beef is advertised for $149.50. It can be paid for over six months in installments of $28.25 per month.

1. How much does the side of beef cost on the install-ment plan? _____

2. What is the cost of the installment plan? _____

3. The cost of the plan is what percent of the advertised cost of the beef? _____

4. If a buyer could get a six-month loan of $150.00 at a 19% annual interest rate for six months, what would the loan cost? _____

5. How much money could be saved by getting a loan instead of paying the installments? _____

A living room set is selling for $1380. It is advertised as hav-ing free financing. You pay $120.75 a month for a year with no money down.

6. What do the payments total by the end of a year? _____

7. What is the difference between the selling price and the total payments for a year? _____

8. The difference is what percent of the selling price? _____

9. What in reality is the finance charge? _____

10. Is this an accurate advertisement? (yes or no) _____

Calculators/Figuring finance charges

People are sometimes not aware of how much they are paying for credit. Any charges on a credit card account that are not paid in full after the monthly statement comes are subject to a finance charge. The **finance charge** is the cost of "borrowing" the money until a later date.

Study this portion of a monthly charge account statement. The finance charge should be the following:

Average daily balance × Monthly rate (1.5%)

$107.81 × .015 = 1.61715, rounded to $1.62

PREVIOUS BALANCE	AVERAGE DAILY BALANCE	FINANCE CHARGE	PURCHASES	PAYMENTS & CREDITS	NEW BALANCE
109.87	107.81	1.62	122.05	50.00	183.54

DATE PAYMENT DUE	10/29/84	TO AVOID ADDITIONAL FINANCE CHARGES, PAY NEW BALANCE BEFORE DATE PAYMENT DUE.

FINANCE CHARGE RATES
PERIODIC RATE PER MONTH   1.5%
ANNUAL PERCENTAGE RATE   18%

Complete the table. Use the 1.5% monthly rate to find the finance charges. Round the answers to the nearest cent.

	Average daily balance	Amount of finance charge	New balance
1.	$47.16	_____	_____
2.	$85.52	_____	_____
3.	$135.40	_____	_____
4.	$220.64	_____	_____
5.	$565.27	_____	_____
6.	$11.10	_____	_____

Life skill/Percents and markup

Store owners buy the goods they sell at wholesale prices
(cost). Then they mark up the prices so that they can make a
profit. The amount of markup is often based on a percent of
the cost. Here is how it's done.

       Cost + Markup = Selling price

Fill in the missing information in this table of prices.

		Wholesale price (Cost)	Markup percent	Markup amount	Selling price
1.	Washer	$205	_____	$112.75	_____
2.	Dryer	$190	37%	_____	_____
3.	TV set	_____	42.5%	$127.50	_____
4.	Freezer	$200	_____	$133.00	_____
5.	Microwave oven	$324	$33 \frac{1}{3}$%	_____	_____
6.	Gas range	_____	$54 \frac{1}{2}$%	$136.25	_____

7. **At the end of the year or season, the store may have a
sale. The sale prices of the appliances are given below.
Find the percent of reduction (decrease) on each appliance. Does the store owner still make a profit?** _____

		Sale price	Savings	Percent of reduction
8.	Washer	$292.33	_____	_____
9.	Dryer	$234.27	_____	_____
10.	TV set	$398.43	_____	_____
11.	Freezer	$305.25	_____	_____
12.	Microwave oven	$408.24	_____	_____
13.	Gas range	$309.00	_____	_____

Practice/Solving proportions

Find each missing number.

1. $\dfrac{3}{4} = \dfrac{60}{n}$ $n =$ _____

2. $\dfrac{5}{8} = \dfrac{n}{88}$ $n =$ _____

3. $\dfrac{51}{n} = \dfrac{17}{1}$ $n =$ _____

4. $\dfrac{n}{48} = \dfrac{7}{8}$ $n =$ _____

5. $\dfrac{19}{38} = \dfrac{20}{n}$ $n =$ _____

6. $\dfrac{16}{80} = \dfrac{n}{60}$ $n =$ _____

7. $\dfrac{21}{n} = \dfrac{5}{15}$ $n =$ _____

8. $\dfrac{n}{16} = \dfrac{40}{64}$ $n =$ _____

9. $\dfrac{75}{225} = \dfrac{50}{n}$ $n =$ _____

10. $\dfrac{12}{96} = \dfrac{n}{64}$ $n =$ _____

11. $\dfrac{11}{n} = \dfrac{32}{96}$ $n =$ _____

12. $\dfrac{n}{144} = \dfrac{7}{84}$ $n =$ _____

13. $\dfrac{28}{56} = \dfrac{39}{n}$ $n =$ _____

14. $\dfrac{15}{n} = \dfrac{39}{65}$ $n =$ _____

15. $\dfrac{52}{91} = \dfrac{n}{49}$ $n =$ _____

16. $\dfrac{n}{27} = \dfrac{45}{81}$ $n =$ _____

Calculators/Solving proportions

Proportions are easy to solve on the calculator. First multiply to find one cross-product. Then divide by the known number in the other cross-product. The answer is the unknown number **n**.

Solve $\dfrac{.25}{.3} = \dfrac{100}{n}$

Press ⊡ ③ ⊠ ① ⓪ ⓪ ⊟ ⊡ ② ⑤ ⊜ .

Your answer should be 120.

Use a calculator to solve these proportions. If an answer has more than two decimal places, round to the nearest hundredth.

1. $\dfrac{459}{17} = \dfrac{n}{800}$

   n = _____

2. $\dfrac{n}{205} = \dfrac{62}{118}$

   n = _____

3. $\dfrac{378}{n} = \dfrac{55}{110}$

   n = _____

4. $\dfrac{.84}{2.54} = \dfrac{.076}{n}$

   n = _____

5. $\dfrac{13.5}{.39} = \dfrac{.28}{n}$

   n = _____

6. $\dfrac{66}{n} = \dfrac{198}{132}$

   n = _____

7. $\dfrac{.79}{1} = \dfrac{n}{1.4}$

   n = _____

8. $\dfrac{n}{42} = \dfrac{328}{120}$

   n = _____

9. $\dfrac{6}{5.05} = \dfrac{.12}{n}$

   n = _____

10. $\dfrac{27}{n} = \dfrac{4.8}{96}$

    n = _____

Practice/Reading a circle graph

Part-time Workers by Field
Total: 6,800,000
85% of the total are women

managers 3.7%

sales 10.1%

clerical 26.7%

professional 19.0%

service 22.9%

other 17.6%

Source: Occupational Outlook Quarterly

Use the graph to answer these questions.

1. In what field do the largest number of part-time workers work? _____

2. How many people work in service jobs part-time? _____

3. What is the difference in percent between people who have sales jobs and people who have professional jobs? _____

4. What is the difference in the number of people working in clerical jobs and service jobs? _____

5. How many women work part-time? _____

Life skill/Reading a double bar graph

A double bar graph shows two sets of information on the same graph. The graph below shows data about both men and women. Read the green part (men) as usual. Read the white part of the bar by subtracting the number for men from the total length of the bar. This gives the number of women workers. The end of both bars gives the total for men and women.

**Employment in Major
Occupational Groups, by Sex**

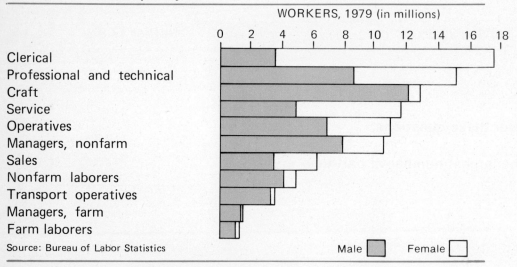

Source: Bureau of Labor Statistics

Use the graph to answer these questions.

1. Do the numbers across the top of the graph stand for hundreds, thousands, or millions? _____

2. How many people work in the clerical field? _____

3. How many men work in the clerical field? _____

4. How many women work in the clerical field? _____

5. What is the percent of women in the clerical field? _____

6. What is the approximate ratio of men to women in the sales field? _____

7. What is the percent of men in the professional field? _____

Life skill/Spotting misleading graphs

Some graphs are not as accurate as they look. Use the checklist as you study a graph to decide if it is misleading.

Checklist
1. Look for the title.
2. Look to see what is being compared.
3. Look for the key to symbols.
4. Look at the numbers across the bottom and/or down the side. Do they make equal jumps?

Study the graph below. Then answer the questions. Circle the letter of each right answer. There may be more than one answer to a problem.

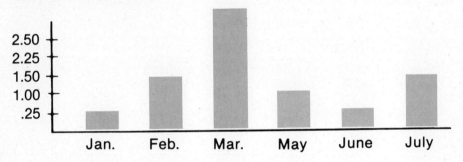

1. What is missing on this graph?
   a. Labels across the bottom.
   b. Labels down the side.
   c. The title.

2. What is incorrect about the months?
   a. The months of the year are not in order.
   b. There is a month missing.
   c. The graph shows only half a year.

3. What is incorrect about the numbers?
   a. There is no sign that the numbers mean dollars.
   b. The numbers do not make equal jumps.
   c. The decimal point is in the wrong place.

4. What is the dollar value for the month of March?
   a. $2.50
   b. $.25
   c. Can't tell.

USE WITH Lesson 33 Bar graphs

Practice/Standard measurement problems

In each problem, write the smaller units as a fraction of the
larger unit. Solve. Give the answer in terms of the larger unit.

1. 4 feet   6 inches $= 4 \frac{6}{12}$ feet
    _____ × 8
                          $= 4 \frac{1}{2}$ feet

    $4 \frac{1}{2} \times 8 = \frac{9}{2} \times \frac{8}{1} = 36$ feet

7. $4 \overline{)5 \text{ pounds} \quad 8 \text{ ounces}}$

2.   3 yards   24 inches
    +   1 yards   12 inches
    _____

8.   7 gallons   1 quart
    −   2 gallons   3 quarts
    _____

3. 12 hours   45 minutes
    _____ × 7

9. $5 \overline{)2 \text{ tons} \quad 1000 \text{ pounds}}$

4.   7 days   15 hours
    +   2 days   18 hours
    _____

10.   3 pints   1 cup
    −   2 pints   1 cup
    _____

5. 6 miles   1320 feet
    _____ × 5

11. $9 \overline{)4 \text{ minutes} \quad 30 \text{ seconds}}$

6.   6 yards   1 feet
    −   3 yards   2 feet
    _____

12.   4 miles   780 yards
    +   8 miles   980 yards
    _____

Practice/Using measurement in landscaping

Solve these problems.

1. Dan works for Hillside Lawn and Care. In the morning he mixes the fertilizer. He uses 27 gallons, 2 quarts of chemical and 58 gallons of water. How much liquid fertilizer does he make?

   _____

2. He checks each order for bushes. One order requires one bush every $6\frac{1}{2}$ feet. How many bushes are needed for a distance of 390 feet?

   _____

3. A six-foot-long planter requires 40 pounds, 10 ounces of potting soil and 1 pound, 8 ounces of dry fertilizer. What will the total weight of the contents of the planter be?

   _____

4. One of Dan's jobs is to trim a 6-foot hedge. He cuts off 1 foot, 5 inches. What is the new height of the hedge?

   _____

5. He uses 1 gallon, 3 quarts of insect spray on each of the 5 flower beds at the park. How much insect spray does he need for the whole job?

   _____

6. A load of top soil for the park weighed 1 ton, 500 pounds. The load was dumped in 5 equal piles. How much soil was in each pile?

   _____

7. In one neighborhood, Dan is going to deliver 47 yards, 1 foot of fencing to each of 8 houses. How much fencing does he need in all?

   _____

Life skill/Working with time zones

The United States, including Hawaii and most of Alaska, is in 5 main time zones. From Eastern Standard Time on the east coast to Pacific Standard Time on the west coast, each time zone to the left, or the west, is one hour earlier. Hawaii and most of Alaska are two hours earlier than Pacific Standard Time. They are two hours earlier because they are separated from the other 48 states and there is another time zone between Pacific Standard Time and Alaska Standard Time.

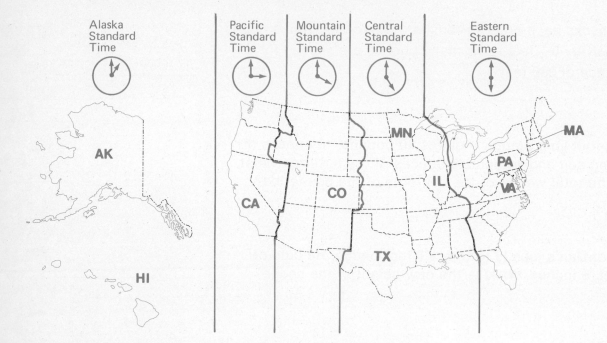

Answer these questions using the information on the map.

1. If it is 6 P.M. in New York, what time is it in California? _____

2. A person in Duluth, MN called Philadelphia, PA at 3:25 P.M. What time was it in Philadelphia? _____

3. A person in California called Hawaii at 6:00 A.M. What time was it in Hawaii? _____

4. Bonnie took a plane from Houston, TX to Boston, MA. The flight took 3 hours and 30 minutes. If she left at 5:50 P.M., what time did she arrive? _____

5. Fred took a charter bus from the Naval Station at Norfolk, VA to San Diego, CA. How many hours did he set back his watch? _____

USE WITH Life skill Reading a time card

Life skill/Comparing costs of health aids

Reading the ads in a newspaper is a good way to comparison shop. Looking for products that have generic labels instead of brand name labels can lead to savings, too. Generic means that the label tells only what the product is and not the brand name.

Study this advertised list of prices.

Generic health aids		Brand name health aids	
Nose drops	150 ml for $3.00	Dr. Jones Nose Drops	100 ml for $2.25
Antiseptic	250 ml for $4.75	Parks Antiseptic	200 ml for $4.00
Bandage tape	10 m for $1.25	Cleancut Bandages	12 m for $1.65
Diaper rash cream	125 mg for $3.75	Baer Diaper Rash Creme	100 mg for $3.25
Alcohol	400 ml for $2.00	Performer Alcohol	200 ml for $.75
Antacid tablets	200 mg for $4.50	Tibb's Antacid	150 mg for $3.30

Compare the prices above. Assume the quality is equal. Find the price per unit. Circle the better buy in each case.

1. Nose drops _____ per ml

   Dr. Jones Nose Drops _____ per ml

2. Antiseptic _____ per ml

   Parks Antiseptic _____ per ml

3. Bandage tape _____ per m

   Cleancut Bandages _____ per m

4. Diaper rash cream _____ per mg

   Baer Creme _____ per mg

5. Alcohol _____ per ml

   Performer Alcohol _____ per ml

6. Antacid tablets _____ per mg

   Tibb's Antacid _____ per mg

7. Go to a store in your area that carries generic products. Compare the prices of three generic items with the prices of the brand name items you usually buy.

Practice/Metric measurement problems

USE WITH Lesson 42

Write each measurement as a decimal of the larger unit.
Solve. Give the answer in terms of the larger unit.

1. 100 meters 50 centimeters × 12
   100.5 meters × 12   _____1206 meters_____

2. 1 liter − 15 milliliters   _____

3. 5 kilograms 45 grams × 8   _____

4. 4 kilometers 250 meters ÷ 5   _____

5. 14 kilograms 50 grams + 18 kilograms 85 grams   _____

6. 1 liter 10 milliliters × 15   _____

7. 18 meters 75 centimeters + 21 meters 40 centimeters   _____

8. 1 kilogram 40 grams − 97 grams   _____

9. 1 liter 250 milliliters + 1 liter 500 milliliters   _____

10. 1 meter 10 centimeters − 50 centimeters   _____

11. 24 liters 30 milliliters ÷ 6   _____

12. 180 kilograms 36 grams ÷ 3   _____

USE WITH Lesson 42 Working with metric measurements

Life skill/Planning a camping trip

When a group decides to camp, hike, hunt, or fish away from home, careful planning is needed. It is important to know distances, weights, and amounts of supplies. Survival may depend on finding the right answers to measurement problems.

Solve these metric measurement problems.

1. The Carvers are planning a camping trip. Each of the three adults will carry a backpack that weighs 12 kilograms, 500 grams. Each of the four children will carry a 4-kilogram pack. What is the total weight of their packs? _____

2. The group plans to hike each day. The first day they will hike 21 kilometers, 500 meters. The second day they will hike 36 kilometers. The third day they will hike 29 kilometers, 500 meters. On the average, how far will they hike each day? _____

3. They are carrying their own drinking water. Each adult is allowed 1 liter, 250 milliliters a day. Each child gets 750 milliliters a day. What is the total amount of drinking water needed for one day? _____

4. For dinner one night they made a stew from a package of dried stew. To make 2 servings, they had to add 450 milliliters of water. How many liters of water did they need to make 10 servings? _____

5. They had a rope 2 meters, 50 centimeters long. They cut it in half. What was the length of each piece? _____

6. By the end of their trip, they had used most of the supplies. The total weight of the packs was now 20 kilograms, 500 grams. What was the weight of the supplies used? _____

Life skill/Preparing your income tax return

The short tax form 1040A is easy to fill out. It is only one page long. You can use it if you do not list deductions and your income is less than $50,000.

Here are part of the 1040A form and portions of the tax tables to use with the practice questions and problems on pages 161 and 162. You need extra copies for page 162.

Portion of 1040A Form

6 Wages, salaries, tips, etc. *(Attach Forms W-2)* . . . . 6 _____ .

7 Interest income *(Complete page 2 if over $400 or you have any All-Savers interest)* . . . . . . 7 _____ .

8a Dividends _____ (Complete page 2 if over $400)   **8b** Exclusion _____ . Subtract line 8b from 8a . . 8c _____ .

9a Unemployment compensation (insurance). Total from Form(s) 1099-UC _____ .

b Taxable amount, if any, from worksheet on page 16 of Instructions . . . . 9b _____ .

10 Add lines 6, 7, 8c, and 9b. This is your total income . . . . 10 _____ .

11 Deduction for a married couple when both work. Complete the worksheet on page 17 . . . . . 11 _____ .

12 Subtract line 11 from line 10. This is your adjusted gross income . . . . 12 _____ .

13 Allowable part of your charitable contributions. Complete the worksheet on page 18 . . . . . 13 _____ .

14 Subtract line 13 from line 12 . . . . 14 _____ .

15 Multiply $1,000 by the total number of exemptions claimed in box 5e . . . . . . 15 _____ .

16 Subtract line 15 from line 14. This is your taxable income . . . . 16 _____ .

17a Partial credit for political contributions. See page 19 . . . . ■ 17a _____ .

b Total Federal income tax withheld, from W-2 form(s). *(If line 6 is more than $32,400, see page 19.)* . . . . 17b _____ .

Stop Here and Sign Below if You Want IRS to Figure Your Tax

c Earned income credit, from worksheet on page 21 . . . . 17c _____ .

18 Add lines 17a, b, and c. These are your total credits and payments . . . . 18 _____

19a Find tax on amount on line 16. Use tax table, pages 26-31 . . . . . 19a _____ .

b Advance EIC payment *(from W-2 form(s))* . . . . 19b _____ .

20 Add lines 19a and 19b. This is your total tax . . . . 20 _____ .

21 If line 18 is larger than line 20, subtract line 20 from line 18. Enter the amount to be **refunded to you** . . . . 21 _____

22 If line 20 is larger than line 18, subtract line 18 from line 20. Enter the **amount you owe.** Attach payment for full amount payable to "Internal Revenue Service." . . . . 22 _____

Tax Table D/Head of Household

If 1040A, line 16, OR 1040EZ, line 7 is—		And you are—			
At least	But less than	Single	Married filing jointly	Married filing separately	Head of a household
			Your tax is—		
5,750	5,800	492	291	589	445
5,800	5,850	500	298	597	452
5,850	5,900	508	305	605	459
5,900	5,950	516	312	613	466
5,950	6,000	524	319	622	473
6,000	6,050	532	326	631	480
6,050	6,100	540	333	641	487
6,100	6,150	548	340	650	494
6,150	6,200	556	347	660	501
6,200	6,250	564	354	669	508

Earned Income Credit Table

If your income is—		Your earned income credit is—
Over	But not over	
7,950	8,000	253
8,000	8,050	247
8,050	8,100	241
8,100	8,150	234
8,150	8,200	228
9,200	9,250	66
9,250	9,300	59
9,300	9,350	53
9,350	9,400	47
9,400	9,450	41
10,000	—	0

NOTE: Get complete forms and instructions from Internal Revenue Service (IRS) to do your taxes. These are only portions of the tables and directions that you need.

Life skill/Preparing your income tax return

Everyone who earned money during the year must file an income tax return. The tax return is an official record of the money you earn and the income tax you pay each year. The form must be sent to the Internal Revenue Service by April 15.

The picture below is a W-2 form. Employers send one to each of their employees. It shows the total amount of money an employee made and the total amount of taxes withheld for the year.

1 Control number	222	2 Employer's State number		
3 Employer's name, address, and ZIP code J & L Corporation 1180 N. Cicero Chicago, Illinois 60614	4 Subtotal □ Correction □ Void □			
	5 Employer's identification number			
	6 Advance EIC payment	7		
8 Employee's social security number	9 Federal income tax withheld 610.00	10 Wages, tips, other compensation 7975.00	11 FICA tax withheld 466.00	12 Total FICA wages 7975.00
13 Employee's name (first, middle, last) and address Marcy Adams 729 Midvale Avenue Chicago, Illinois 60640	14 Pension plan coverage? Yes/No No	15	16 FICA tips	
	18 State income tax withheld 253.23	19 State wages, tips, etc. 7975.00	20 Name of state Illinois	
	21 Local income tax withheld	22 Local wages, tips, etc.	23 Name of locality	

Copy B To be filed with employee's FEDERAL tax return
This information is being furnished to the Internal Revenue Service.

Read the W-2 form above and answer these questions.

1. What is Marcy Adams' gross income? _____

2. What is the total amount of federal income tax withheld? _____

3. What is the total amount of state income tax withheld? _____

4. What is the total amount of FICA (social security) tax withheld? _____

5. What is the total amount of money Ms. Adams actually received from her company to spend during the year? _____

Life skill/Preparing your income tax return

Marcy Adams is an unmarried head of household with one child. She claimed 2 exemptions. Last year she earned $7975. Put that amount on line 6 of the income tax form. She has already paid $610 in Federal taxes. Put that amount on line 17b. Put zeros on lines 7, 8c, 9b, 11, 13, 17a, and 19b.

- What is her adjusted gross income? Add lines 6, 7, 8c, and 9b.) Put the answer on lines 10, 12, and 14. $7975.00

- Multiply the number of exemptions by $1000. Put the answer on line 15. $2000.00

- To find her taxable income, subtract line 15 from line 14. Put the answer on line 16. $5975.00

- Use the table to find her Earned Income Credit. Put the answer on line 17c. $253.00

- Total lines 17a, 17b, and 17c. Put the answer on line 18. $863.00

- Use the tax table to find her income tax based on her taxable income. Put the answer on lines 19a and 20. $473.00

- Subtract line 20 from line 18. Put the answer on line 21. This is what will be refunded to her. $390.00

Fill out a 1040A form for each of the following.

Hal Kaufman has 2 children. As head of household he claimed 3 exemptions. He earned $9235 last year (line 6). He has already paid $595 in taxes (line 17b). Put zeros on lines 7, 8c, 9b, 11, 13, 17a, and 19b.

1. What is his adjusted gross income? (line 12) _____
2. How much is allowed for his exemptions? (line 15) _____
3. What is his taxable income? (line 16) _____
4. What is his Earned Income Credit? (line 17c) _____
5. What is the total of lines 17a, 17b, and 17c? (line 18) _____
6. How much income tax is due? (lines 19a and 20) _____
7. How much is his refund? (line 21) _____

Juana Martinez is a single head of household with 3 children. She claimed 4 exemptions. She earned $10,055 last year (line 6). She has already paid $495 in taxes (line 17b). Put zeros on lines 7, 8c, 9b, 11, 13, 17a, and 19b. Because she has earned over $10,000 she is not allowed an Earned Income Credit. Put zero on line 17c.

8. What is her adjusted gross income? (line 12) _____
9. How much is allowed for her exemptions? (line 15) _____
10. What is her taxable income? (line 16) _____
11. What is the total of lines 17a, 17b, and 17c? (line 18) _____
12. What is her income tax? (lines 19a and 20) _____
13. What is her refund? (line 21) _____

Sample pre-employment test/page 1

Fill in the information requested.

Name	Number and street	City

State	Zip code	Social Security number
		  - -
			Birthdate
			  / /

Job applying for:	FOR OFFICE USE ONLY
	Time begun Time ended Total

Blacken the space under the letter of the correct answer to each problem.

Example

$\frac{1}{2}$ of 44 is

a. 88   **c.** 10
b. 22   **d.** 20

a b c d
|| ▓ || ||

1. What is next in the series: 2, 6, 10, 14, 18, _____
    a. 36   **c.** 22
    b. 18   **d.** 24

    a b c d
    || || || ||

2. The maximum load for a freight elevator is 1890 pounds. How many 18-pound crates can be loaded onto the elevator safely?
    a. 105   **c.** 108
    b. 34,020   **d.** 95

    a b c d
    || || || ||

3. What shape could this paper take if it were folded at the dotted lines?

    a.   **b.**   **c.**   **d.**

    a b c d
    || || || ||

4. A machine produces 75 centimeters of film a second. What will be the length produced in an hour?
    a. 45 meters   **c.** 270,000 meters
    b. 4500 meters   **d.** 2700 meters

    a b c d
    || || || ||

5. What is 25% of 48?
   a. 12   **c.** 16
   b. 144   **d.** 20

   a   b   c   d
   || || || ||

6. Each can of machine oil contains 3 gallons and 2 quarts.
   The factory uses 8 cans a day. How much oil is used
   in a 7-day week?
   a. 49 gal.   **c.** 168 gal.
   b. 196 gal.   **d.** 120 gal.

   a   b   c   d
   || || || ||

Use the graph to answer questions 7–10.

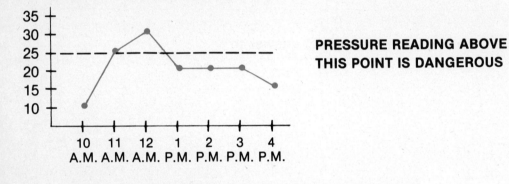

PRESSURE READING ABOVE
THIS POINT IS DANGEROUS

7. At what time did the reading go above the danger line?
   a. 11 A.M.   **c.** 1 P.M.
   b. 12 A.M.   **d.** 2 P.M.

   a   b   c   d
   || || || ||

8. When did the machine have its lowest reading?
   a. 10 A.M.   **c.** 1 P.M.
   b. 12 A.M.   **d.** 2 P.M.

   a   b   c   d
   || || || ||

9. What was the reading at 4 P.M.?
   a. 10   **c.** 20
   b. 15   **d.** 25

   a   b   c   d
   || || || ||

10. What is the average reading for the time period shown?
    a. 140   **c.** 20
    b. 15   **d.** 10

    a   b   c   d
    || || || ||

Answers

Lesson 1/page 2
1. 8.63
2. 1.68
3. 11.16
4. 787.23
5. .09
6. 459.191
7. 1023.05
8. 567.03
9. 16.543
10. 1033.88

Lesson 2/page 3
1. 13.59
2. 1.177
3. 2.2533
4. 34.506
5. 10.5041
6. 2306.5082
7. 32.791
8. 976.8
9. 161.633
10. .55
11. 82.65
12. .9610755

Lesson 3/page 4
1. 600
2. 8.1
3. 40
4. .087
5. 500
6. 28
7. .45
8. 50
9. .231
10. 300
11. 666.66
12. 7100
13. 70
14. .1145
15. 30

Lesson 4/pages 5, 6
1. $\frac{1}{12}$
2. $8\frac{1}{4}$
3. $11\frac{1}{2}$
4. $\frac{1}{20}$
5. $10\frac{2}{3}$
6. $17\frac{1}{3}$
7. $\frac{15}{25}$
8. $\frac{9}{81}$
9. $\frac{45}{55}$
10. $\frac{49}{56}$
11. $\frac{60}{72}$
12. $\frac{6}{39}$
13. 9
14. 20
15. 16
16. 60
17. 18
18. 60
19. $8\frac{3}{2}$
20. $8\frac{12}{12}$
21. $46\frac{11}{8}$
22. $5\frac{3}{3}$
23. $20\frac{15}{8}$
24. $18\frac{3}{2}$
25. $4\frac{2}{5}$
26. $7\frac{1}{2}$
27. 9
28. 1
29. $5\frac{1}{3}$
30. 1
31. $\frac{27}{5}$
32. $\frac{100}{3}$
33. $\frac{59}{8}$
34. $\frac{29}{3}$
35. $\frac{50}{3}$
36. $\frac{25}{3}$

Lesson 5/page 8
1. $3\frac{3}{5}$
2. $12\frac{3}{10}$
3. $13\frac{7}{12}$
4. $28\frac{13}{33}$
5. $10\frac{5}{12}$
6. $52\frac{11}{12}$
7. $11\frac{1}{3}$
8. 3
9. $13\frac{7}{8}$
10. 17
11. $20\frac{1}{72}$
12. $7\frac{31}{35}$
13. $5\frac{3}{8}$
14. $17\frac{13}{35}$
15. $22\frac{2}{33}$
16. 13
17. $18\frac{26}{33}$
18. $9\frac{3}{10}$
19. c
20. a

Lesson 6/page 9
1. $\frac{1}{6}$
2. $1\frac{1}{3}$
3. $\frac{4}{39}$
4. $3\frac{1}{8}$
5. $12\frac{1}{2}$
6. $\frac{7}{40}$
7. 18
8. $1\frac{3}{5}$
9. 124
10. $9\frac{3}{8}$
11. 450
12. 135

Lesson 7/page 10
1. 1
2. 44
3. $\frac{3}{4}$
4. $\frac{2}{3}$
5. $1\frac{1}{2}$
6. 20
7. $\frac{1}{4}$
8. 141
9. $1\frac{2}{9}$
10. $\frac{1}{8}$
11. 15
12. 2

Lesson 8/page 11
1. .1
2. 1.5
3. $.16\frac{2}{3}$
4. .4
5. $5.37\frac{1}{2}$ or 5.375
6. $.66\frac{2}{3}$
7. .75
8. 11.9
9. $\frac{1}{8}$
10. $\frac{1}{4}$
11. $5\frac{1}{100}$
12. $\frac{1}{5}$
13. $\frac{17}{20}$
14. $6\frac{1}{8}$
15. $\frac{3}{2500}$
16. $\frac{3}{1000}$

Lesson 9/page 12
1. $\frac{3}{4}$
2. .3
3. 1.1
4. .85
5. .4
6. .09
7. .009
8. .49
9. $2\frac{4}{5}$
10. $\frac{1}{8}$
11. .09 $\frac{1}{5}$ .9
12. $\frac{3}{8}$ $\frac{5}{9}$ .6

Pretest/Unit 2/page 13
1. 25%
2. 75%
3. 100%
4. .25
5. 2.45
6. .01
7. $.66\frac{2}{3}$
8. .77
9. .0008
10. $\frac{9}{10}$
11. $\frac{1}{6}$
12. $2\frac{22}{25}$
13. $\frac{17}{25}$
14. $\frac{1}{200}$
15. $\frac{1}{25}$
16. $33\frac{1}{3}$%
17. 175%
18. 4210%
19. 100%
20. .82%
21. 20%
22. $\frac{1}{4}$, 30%, .75, $\frac{4}{5}$
23. 15%, $\frac{1}{6}$, .33, $\frac{5}{8}$
24. .04, 18%, 2, 2.1

Lesson 10/page 16
1. a. a bottle of syrup
   b. It means the whole bottle is filled with natural maple syrup.
2. a. a garment (sweater)
   b. It means the fabric is all wool.
3. a. a dollar bill
   b. It means that the whole dollar was spent.

4. 100%
5. 100%
6. 100%
7. 100%

Lesson 11/pages 17–19
1. 98%
2. 2%
3. 100%
4. 100%
5. 68%
6. 168%
7. 100%
8. 4%
9. 104%
10. $99\frac{1}{4}$%
11. $\frac{3}{4}$%
12. 100%
13. 100% is one whole unit.
14. Less than 100% is less than one whole unit.
15. Less than 1% is less than $\frac{1}{100}$ of a whole unit.
16. More than 100% is more than one whole unit.

Life skill/page 21
Answers will vary.

Lesson 12/page 22
1. $\frac{1}{2}$
2. 50¢
3. $.50
4. 50%
5. $\frac{1}{10}$
6. 10¢
7. $.10
8. 75%

Lesson 13/page 23
1. .67
2. 1.98
3. .02
4. .59
5. 9.99
6. $.16\frac{2}{3}$
7. .005
8. .456
9. .3708
10. .00076
11. $.12\frac{1}{2}$

12. .44
13. .07
14. $.33\frac{1}{3}$
15. $.08\frac{1}{7}$
16. .05
17. 1.5

Lesson 14/page 24
1. 35%
2. 1%
3. 900%
4. .2%
5. $33\frac{1}{3}$%
6. 90%
7. 125%
8. 100%
9. 10%
10. $16\frac{2}{3}$%
11. 55%
12. 80%
13. 250%
14. .6%
15. $8\frac{1}{2}$%
16. .5%
17. 80%

Lesson 15/page 25
1. $\frac{9}{10}$ 10. $\frac{3}{5}$
2. $7\frac{3}{4}$ 11. $1\frac{1}{2}$
3. $\frac{1}{3}$ 12. $\frac{1}{6}$
4. 1   13. $\frac{17}{20}$
5. $1\frac{9}{10}$ 14. $2\frac{13}{20}$
6. $\frac{7}{8}$ 15. $\frac{5}{6}$
7. $\frac{11}{50}$ 16. $\frac{1}{4}$
8. $1\frac{2}{3}$ 17. $\frac{7}{10}$
9. $\frac{19}{60}$

Lesson 16/page 26
1. 40%
2. 25%
3. 4%
4. $44\frac{4}{9}$%
5. 290%
6. 2%
7. 3.3%
8. $3\frac{1}{3}$%
9. 175%
10. 87.5% or $87\frac{1}{2}$%
11. 13.4%
12. 525%
13. $16\frac{2}{3}$%
14. $8\frac{1}{3}$%

Lesson 17/page 27
1. $\frac{10}{100}$ .10
2. $\frac{9}{100}$ .09
3. $\frac{2}{100}$ .02
4. 2%; .09; $\frac{1}{10}$
5. 1   1.00
6. $\frac{1}{3}$ $.33\frac{1}{3}$
7. $1\frac{1}{2}$ 1.50
8. $.33\frac{1}{3}$; 100%; $1\frac{1}{2}$
9. $\frac{330}{1000}$ .330
10. $\frac{33}{1000}$ .033
11. $\frac{300}{1000}$ .300
12. 3.3%; $\frac{3}{10}$; .33

Posttest/Unit 2/page 28
1. 16%
2. 84%
3. 100%
4. $\frac{19}{20}$
5. .95
6. 1
7. 100%
8. .125
9. 12.5% $12\frac{1}{2}$
10. $2\frac{4}{5}$
11. 2.8
12. $\frac{3}{500}$
13. .6%
14. .002
15. .2%
16. $\frac{2}{125}$
17. .016
18. $\frac{1}{6}$
19. $16\frac{2}{3}$%
20. .5
21. 50%
22. $\frac{5}{6}$ .83   8.4%
23. .5 $\frac{1}{5}$ .11%
24. .55 $\frac{1}{2}$ .55%
25. .35 $\frac{1}{3}$ 33%
26. 6.3   63% $\frac{6}{10}$
27. 4.55 $4\frac{1}{2}$ 4.2
28. 20%
29. 78%
30. .0093

Pretest/Unit 3/page 29
1. 440   6. 9000
2. 30
3. $8\frac{1}{3}$%   7. $66\frac{2}{3}$%
4. 750   8. 200
5. 6000   9. .08
          10. 300%

11. $100.00
12. $300.00
13. $19.50
14. 3%
15. $328.50

Lesson 18/page 30
1. part 30; percent ?
   whole 50
2. part 16; percent 60
   whole ?
3. part 10; percent 30
   whole ?
4. part 4; percent ?
   whole 20
5. part ?; percent 25
   whole 80
6. part 22; percent 1
   whole ?
7. part ?; percent 9
   whole 81
8. part 45; percent ?
   whole 90
9. part 2; percent 1
   whole ?
10. part ?; percent 45
    whole 5

Lesson 19/pages 31–32
1. 200   9. 7000
2. 560   10. 40
3. 513.33   11. a
4. 285.71   12. d
5. 18   13. b
6. 4   14. a
7. 17,600   15. c
8. 800

Life skill/page 33
3. $1.24   8. $5.97
4. $1.86   9. $14.88
5. $10.60   10. $22.32
6. $15.90   11. $4.18
7. $3.98   12. $6.27

Lesson 20/pages 34–35
1. 13.75   10. 891
2. 500   11. d
3. 255.2   12. b
4. 4500   13. a
5. 1.1   14. a
6. 41.4   15. d
7. 738.139
8. 12
9. 2.24

Life skill/page 37
1. $60.00   6. $1.50
2. $180.00   7. $3.50
3. $.37   8. $17.50
4. $1.48   9. $206.38
5. $8.88

Lesson 21/pages 38–39
1. $33\frac{1}{3}$%   4. 50%
2. 10%   5. $33\frac{1}{3}$%
3. 50%   6. 300%

7. 40%   11. d
8. $12\frac{1}{2}$%   12. b
               13. b
9. $33\frac{1}{3}$%   14. c
10. 20%   15. a

Life skill/page 41
1. $1120.00
2. 25%
3. $12\frac{1}{2}$%
4. 10%
5. 20%
6. .5%
7. 8.93%
8. $258.40

Lesson 22/pages 42–43
1. whole 300
2. percent $33\frac{1}{3}$%
3. part 124.3
4. whole 295
5. percent 25%
6. part 890
7. whole 1800
8. percent $11\frac{1}{9}$%
9. part 355.25
10. whole 2793
11. 20%   21. 400%
12. 52.8   22. 400
13. 300   23. 8000
14. 1%   24. 72
15. 0.125   25. 10%
16. 600   26. 60
17. 2400   27. 90%
18. 5%   28. 60%
19. 1100
20. 144

Life skill/page 44
1. 12%
2. 4.1%
3. 3.4%
4. 0.34%
5. $3195.00
6. $2510.00
7. $2873.00
8. $3765.00
9. $.55
10. $1.76
11. $1.43
12. $8.69

Posttest/Unit 3/page 45
1. 550%   10. $11\frac{1}{9}$%
2. 570
3. 1800   11. 500
             12. 38
4. $33\frac{1}{3}$%   13. 26
             14. 14
5. 428.4   15. 450
6. 2912.5
7. $66\frac{2}{3}$%   16. $88\frac{8}{9}$%
8. .00375
9. 484

Pretest/Unit 4/page 46
1. $204.00
2. $30.00
3. $33\frac{1}{3}$%
4. $88.00
5. $430.92
6. $518.92
7. 17.94%
8. $54.00
9. $494.00
10. $24.92

Lesson 23/page 48
1. $19.50
2. $18.10
3. $334.40
4. $11.50
5. $96.75
6. $20.28
7. $3409.25
8. $400.59
9. $368.75
10. $239.69

Lesson 24/pages 51–52
1. $25.00
2. $21.25
3. $30.75
4. $292.50
5. $24.75
6. $150.50
7. $250.80
8. $22.50
9. $390.00
10. $312.00
11. $502.40
12. $1218.30
13. $24.60
14. $729.12
15. $14.73
16. $15.63
17. $166.10
18. $109.67
19. c
20. a
21. b
22. b

Lesson 25/pages 54–55
1. $59.85
2. $399.60
3. $459.45
4. $35.91
5. $24.54
6. $118.75
7. $420.00
8. $538.75
9. $47.50
10. $16.25
11. $15.04
12. $198.00
13. $213.04
14. $14.25
15. $8.79

Lesson 26/pages 56–58
1. increase, $12\frac{1}{2}$%
2. 18%   8. 30%
3. 28%   9. 17%
4. 43%   10. 2300%
5. 22%   11. 9%
6. 40%   12. 7%
7. 33%

Posttest/Unit 4/page 59
1. $10.50
2. $667.47
3. 45%
4. $22.00
5. $310.00
6. 12.7%
7. $30.25
8. $305.25
9. $4.75
10. $.0285 ($28\frac{1}{2}$¢)

Practicing for mastery
Unit 5/pages 60–62
1. .15
2. $\frac{3}{20}$
3. 50%
4. $\frac{1}{2}$
5. 25%
6. .25
7. $.33\frac{1}{3}$
8. $\frac{1}{3}$
9. $83\frac{1}{3}$%
10. $\frac{5}{6}$
11. 1.15
12. $1\frac{3}{20}$
13. 1%
14. $\frac{1}{100}$
15. 420%
16. 4.2
17. .5%
18. .005
19. 1
20. 1
21. 890
22. 16.66
23. 2%
24. 353.3
25. 38.5
26. $33\frac{1}{3}$%
27. 39.39
28. 37.5
29. 5%
30. 500%
31. 142 or 143 people.
32. 2900 Votes
33. 12%
34. $52.50

35. $897.00
36. $17.88
37. $728.00
38. $77.50
39. $1794.00
40. $22.35
41. $72.80
42. $16\frac{2}{3}$%
43. 15%
44. 20%
45. $18\frac{3}{4}$%
46. $15.00
47. $159.00
48. $174.00

Part 1 test/pages 64–66
1. 50%
2. .5
3. .16
4. $\frac{4}{25}$
5. 75%
6. $\frac{3}{4}$
7. 921%
8. $9\frac{21}{100}$
9. $66\frac{2}{3}$%
10. $.66\frac{2}{3}$
11. 95%
12. $\frac{19}{20}$
13. $33\frac{1}{3}$%
14. $.33\frac{1}{3}$
15. 83%
16. $\frac{83}{100}$
17. .14
18. $\frac{7}{50}$
19. .005
20. $\frac{1}{200}$
21. 850%
22. 570
23. 1728
24. $33\frac{1}{3}$%
25. 2196
26. $66\frac{2}{3}$%
27. .00375
28. 7237.5
29. 989 votes
30. $35.29
31. 9%
32. $624
33. $224.40
34. $17,398.50
35. $16.25
36. $16\frac{2}{3}$%
37. 6.6%
38. $437.55

39. 16.7%
40. $52.50
41. $427.50
42. $10.05

Pretest/Unit 6/page 69
1. 75
2. 51
3. $\frac{2}{3}$
4. 6
5. 198
6. 1
7. b
8. a
9. d
10. a
11. b

Lesson 27/page 72
1. 2:1
2. 1:10,000,000
3. 1:25
4. 25:1
5. 8:1
6. 24:1
7. 20:80 or 1:4
8. 1:3
9. $\frac{125}{275}$ or $\frac{5}{11}$
10. $\frac{5}{65}$ or $\frac{1}{13}$
11. $\frac{336}{6}$ or $\frac{56}{1}$
12. $\frac{2}{5}$
13. $\frac{3}{1}$
14. $\frac{24}{1284}$ or $\frac{2}{107}$
15. $\frac{45}{55}$ or $\frac{9}{11}$

Lesson 28/page 73
1. 12:18 :: 44:66
   $\frac{12}{18} = \frac{44}{66}$
2. 27:54 :: 45:90
   $\frac{27}{54} = \frac{45}{90}$
3. 9:81 :: 15:135
   $\frac{9}{81} = \frac{15}{135}$
4. 10:100 :: 100:1000
   $\frac{10}{100} = \frac{100}{1000}$
5. 150:300 :: 75:150
   $\frac{150}{300} = \frac{75}{150}$
6. 99:1 :: 990:10
   $\frac{99}{1} = \frac{990}{10}$
7. 348:58 :: 162:27
   $\frac{348}{58} = \frac{162}{27}$
8. 17:51 :: 1:3
   $\frac{17}{51} = \frac{1}{3}$
9. 55:200 :: 110:400
   $\frac{55}{200} = \frac{110}{400}$

Lesson 29/page 75
1. 21 parks
2. 12.8 gallons
3. 3262 miles
4. 276 parts
5. 2 new cooks
6. 623 pancakes

Life skill/page 77
1. $2.00
2. $2.16
3. $5.13
4. $1.98
5. $.82
6. $.40
7. $4.92
8. $6.56
9. $3.64

Lesson 30/page 78
1. $\frac{1}{4}$
2. 7744
3. 200
4. $\frac{3}{4}$
5. 13.125
6. $\frac{11}{18}$

Life skill/page 79
1. 1 inch
2. $\frac{3}{4}$ inch
3. 6 miles
4. 7.5 miles

Life skill/page 81
1. $\frac{3}{8}$ pound
2. $\frac{1}{4}$ pound
3. 3 Tablespoons
4. $2\frac{1}{4}$ ounces
5. 6 ounces
6. 12 ounces
7. $\frac{3}{4}$ teaspoon
8. $1\frac{1}{8}$ teaspoons
9. $\frac{3}{8}$ teaspoon
10. $1\frac{1}{2}$ teaspoons
11. $1\frac{1}{4}$ pounds
12. $\frac{5}{6}$ pound
13. 10 Tablespoons
14. $7\frac{1}{2}$ ounces
15. 20 ounces
16. 40 ounces
17. $2\frac{1}{2}$ teaspoons
18. $3\frac{3}{4}$ teaspoons
19. $1\frac{1}{4}$ teaspoons
20. 5 teaspoons

Posttest/Unit 6/page 83
1. 5
2. 125
3. $1\frac{1}{2}$
4. .1
5. 106
6. 3
7. a
8. d
9. b
10. c
11. a

Pretest/Unit 7
pages 84–86
1. 6%
2. 1%
3. 17,655,440
4. 15,247,880
5. 1:6
6. 13,642,840
7. 9,500
8. 13,000
9. 8,500
10. 1,500
11. 37%
12. 19:25
13. 27,000,000
14. $\frac{45}{18}$ or $\frac{5}{2}$
15. 26,000,000
16. $\frac{70}{44}$ or $\frac{35}{22}$
17. 55%, 144%
18. women

Lesson 31/pages 87–88
1. 100%
2. 30%
3. 20%
4. $2375.00
5. $760.00
6. $1140.00
7. $1,900.00
8. $\frac{5}{6}$ or 5:6
9. $1\frac{1}{2}$
10. 5
11. 30%
12. 25%
13. 15%
14. 20%
15. 10%
16. 221,800,000
17. population and age
18. 26%
19. 10%
20. Birth–19 Years
21. 55–64 and 45–54
22. 35–44 and 65+
23. 70,976,000
24. 57,668,000
25. 24,398,000

Lesson 32/pages 90–91
1. 1960, 1970, 1980
2. 100,000
3. 1,864,000
4. 2,906,000
5. 2,756,600
6. 1864:2906 or 932:1453
7. 148% (Rounded off)
8. 27,566:18,640 or 13,783:9320
9. $100,000.00
10. $750,000.00
11. $900,000.00
12. $650,000.00
13. $100,000.00
14. 3:4
15. 120%
16. $150,000.00

Lesson 33/pages 92–93
1. $9,500.00
2. $15,000.00
3. $2,600.00
4. $3,900.00
5. 500%
6. 5:1
7. $3,500.00
8. $3,000.00
9. Salesperson
10. 63.15%
11. 60%
12. 72%

Lesson 34/page 95
1. Farm
2. 5,000,000
3. 71%
4. 18,000,000
5. 138%
6. 4% per year
7. 11,000,000
8. 47%
9. 1.36% increase per year

Lesson 35/pages 97–98
1. dial-direct and operator-assisted
2. weekday, evening, night and weekend
3. station-to-station, person-to-person
4. 1-minute
5. 1-minute
6. no
7. $1.55
8. $1.45
9. $3.49
10. $8.48
11. $2.97
12. 49:78
13. Years
14. Budget Items
15. The changing values of a dollar
16. Consumer Price Index
17. $3.84
18. $1.50
19. $1.17

20. $1.09
21. 92%
22. 78%
23. 17:20

Posttest/Unit 7
pages 99–101
1. 27,000
2. 44,000
3. 71,000
4. 27:44
5. cooks and chefs
6. 79:71
7. 50%
8. 34:23
9. 37,000
10. circle graph
11. 24,915,550
12. 10,192,725
13. 1,585,535
14. 11:83.4
15. $\frac{1}{250}$
16. $\frac{7}{1000}$
17. 1970–1975
18. 200,000
19. 50,000
20. $133\frac{1}{3}\%$
21. 20%
22. 7:4

Pretest/Unit 8
pages 102–103
1. 5.12 meters
2. $3\frac{3}{4}$ lb.
3. $4\frac{1}{4}$ hours
4. 1.25l
5. 17 quart jars
6. 850 ml
7. 255 grams
8. 1 yd. 22 in.
9. $.60
10. $.55
11. $.89
12. $.81
13. 5.83\frac{1}{3}$
14. $7.90
15. 2.48$\frac{3}{4}$
16. $3.05

Lesson 36/page 105
1. A
2. B
3. C
4. C
5. C
6. A
7. B
8. C
9. A
10. B
11. C
12. B
13. A

168

14. C 22. G
15. C 23. I
16. C 24. A
17. A 25. D
18. B 26. C
19. A 27. E
20. F 28. H
21. J 29. B

Lesson 37/ page 106
1. 29 qt.
2. 3 days
3. 34,000 lb.
4. 180 min.
5. 156 in.
6. 52 oz.

Lesson 38/ pages 107–109
1. $\frac{3}{4}$
2. $2\frac{11}{12}$
3. $\frac{1}{20}$
4. $3\frac{1}{2}$
5. $\frac{5}{6}$
6. $12\frac{1}{4}$
7. $\frac{3}{4}$
8. $2\frac{1}{3}$
9. $5\frac{1}{4}$
10. $\frac{1}{3}$
11. $\frac{1}{2}$ mi.
12. $17\frac{1}{2}$ lb.
13. $9\frac{1}{3}$ yd.
14. $\frac{1}{4}$ hr.
15. 10 hr.
16. $3\frac{3}{4}$ min.
17. $\frac{1}{3}$ ft.
18. $7\frac{6}{7}$ week
19. $\frac{5}{6}$ min.
20. 3 qt.
21. $1\frac{1}{3}$ yd.
22. $1\frac{1}{2}$ mi.
23. $9\frac{3}{4}$ days
24. 46.35 T.
25. 14 oz. or $\frac{7}{8}$ lb.
26. 3 T.
27. 6 pt.
28. $7\frac{1}{2}$ hr.
29. $23\frac{3}{4}$ gal.
30. 18.5 mi.
31. $3\frac{1}{2}$ qt.

Life skill/ page 111
1. $97\frac{1}{2}$ ft.
2. $92\frac{1}{2}$ ft.

3. 20 ft.
4. 68 ft.
5. $4\frac{2}{9}$ ft.
6. $8\frac{1}{3}$ ft.
7. $2\frac{1}{2}$ in.

Life skill/ page 113
1. 3 hr.
2. $4\frac{1}{2}$ hr. or 4 hr. 30 min.
3. $6\frac{2}{3}$ hr. or 6 hr. 40 min.
4. $7\frac{1}{2}$ hr. or 7 hr. 30 min.
5. $4\frac{1}{3}$ hr. or 4 hr. 20 min.
6. $8\frac{1}{2}$ hr. or 8 hr. 30 min.

Life skill/ page 115
1. $12\frac{1}{2}$ hr. or 12 hr. 30 min.
2. $6\frac{1}{4}$ hr. or 6 hr. 15 min.
3. $37\frac{1}{2}$ hr. or 37 hr. 30 min.
4. 9 hr.
5. 54 hr.
6. 10:00 A.M.
7. 11:45 P.M.
8. 63 hr.

Lesson 39/ page 117
1. ($.47\frac{1}{4}$)
2. $.49\frac{1}{3}$
3. ($.49\frac{1}{2}$)
4. $.64
5. $.59
6. ($.55$)
7. $.02\frac{1}{2}$
8. ($.02\frac{1}{4}$)
9. (1.48)
10. $1.56

Lesson 40/ page 118
1. 104°F or 40°C
2. 32°F or 0°C
3. 65°F or 18°C
4. 212°F or 100°C
5. 41°F or 5°C
6. 77°F or 25°C

Lesson 41/ page 119
1. 37,000
2. 3,700,000
3. 37,000,000
4. .142
5. 142,000
6. .00005 km
7. .05 m
8. 50 mm
9. 34,005,000
10. 34,005,000,000
11. .027 k*l*
12. 27,000 m*l*

Lesson 42/ pages 120–121
1. 5.692 *l*
2. 79.052 m
3. 46.056 km
4. 9.798 km
5. 6.025 k*l*
6. 78.45 m
7. 22.992 g
8. 59.026 kg
9. 11.546 *l*
10. 327.925 k*l*
11. .266 m
12. 141.235 m*l*
13. 46.5 m*l*
14. 1.689 *l*
15. 92.000066 kg
16. 22.5 kg
17. .4 *l*
18. 2.7 km
19. 3.843 g
20. b
21. b
22. b
23. b
24. a
25. a
26. b

Life skill/ page 122
1. 18.75 m
2. 25.5 m
3. $10.20
4. 18.48 m
5. $46.20
6. 1050 g

Life skill/ page 123
1. ($.0022\frac{1}{2}$)
2. $.0032
3. ($.0014$)
4. $.0016
5. ($.0097$)
6. $.01
7. ($.02$)
8. $.025

Life skill/ page 125
1. 250 m*l*
2. 5 kg
3. 25
4. 29 kg
5. 275 m*l*
6. 9.36 kg
7. 27.3 kg
8. 156

Post test/ Unit 8
pages 126–127
1. 26.125 km
2. $11\frac{3}{4}$ lb.
3. $\frac{1}{2}$ hr.
4. 9.896 *l*
5. $3\frac{1}{2}$ ft.
6. 52.25 *l*
7. 1830.475 *l*
8. 3.6 kg

9. ($.0007$)
10. $.008
11. $.50
12. ($.45$)
13. ($.79$)
14. $.80
15. $.47\frac{1}{2}$
16. ($.45$)

Practicing for mastery
Unit 9/ pages 128–130
1. $225.00
2. 25
3. 45
4. 50
5. 135
6. 3
7. $18.00
8. $\frac{3}{4}$ gal.
9. $23\frac{15}{16}$ lb.
10. 11.25 kg
11. 4.5 m
12. 18 hr.
13. B
14. B
15. B
16. B
17. clerical workers
18. 10,000,000
19. farm workers
20. 200,000
21. 4,700,000
22. 3:5
23. 1,400,000

Part 2 test/ pages 131–133
1. $55.08
2. 16.2 gal. or $16\frac{1}{5}$ gal.
3. $4500.00
4. 14 customers
5. 7:1
6. $31\frac{1}{2}$ mi.
7. $51.00
8. $\frac{3}{4}$ gal. or 3 qt.
9. 34 hr.
10. $157\frac{2}{3}$ ft. or 157 ft. 8 in.
11. 120 g or .12 kg
12. 93.75 g
13. B
14. B
15. A
16. B
17. clerical workers
18. 17,600,000
19. private household workers
20. 1,100,000
21. 128:47 or 64:23
22. 14,900,000
23. 2,200,000

Life skill/page 136
1. 20 miles
2. 10 miles
3. 50 miles
4. 95 units
5. $16\frac{2}{3}$ watts
6. 300 units

Practice/page 137
1. $\frac{1}{2}$, .5
2. $\frac{1}{3}$, $33\frac{1}{3}\%$
3. 10%, .1
4. $1\frac{7}{20}$, 135%
5. $\frac{1}{6}$, $.16\frac{2}{3}$
6. 62.5%, .625
7. $\frac{1}{200}$, $\frac{1}{2}\%$ or .5%
8. .2% or $\frac{1}{5}\%$, .002
9. $\frac{3}{200}$, .015
10. 99%, .99
11. $25\frac{57}{100}$, .25.57
12. $\frac{9}{10}$, 90%

Life skill/page 138
1. 5
2. 8,000,000
3. a. 100
   b. 1600
4. a. 18 miles/gallon
   b. 30 miles/gallon
5. a. 219,484,000
   b. 23,500,000

Life skill/page 139
2. $30,900, $1,081.50
3. $40,320, $1,411.20
4. $29,940, $748.50
5. $33,240, $831.00
6. $34,800, $957.00
7. $42,000, $1,260.00
8. $53,400, $1,335.00

Life skill/page 140
1. $43\frac{3}{4}\%$, $4.50
2. 50%, $0.75
3. 25%, $3.75
4. $32\frac{1}{2}\%$, $6.50
5. 45%, $15.84
6. $33\frac{1}{3}\%$, $23.30
7. 41%, $17.11
8. $16\frac{2}{3}\%$, $0.85

Practice/page 141
1. 65.6
2. 120
3. $33\frac{1}{3}\%$

4. 510
5. 582
6. 50%
7. .005
8. 75
9. 50%
10. 1.7
11. 2.5
12. $33\frac{1}{3}\%$
13. 94
14. 500
15. $8\frac{1}{3}\%$
16. 2100
17. 3
18. 1
19. 20%
20. 5600
21. $33\frac{1}{3}\%$
22. 2.97
23. 1.2%
24. $66\frac{2}{3}\%$

Life Skill/page 142
Precinct 1 45%, 55%
Precinct 2 4,080, 3,920
Precinct 3 2,500, $66\frac{2}{3}\%$
Precinct 4 11,250, 38%
Precinct 5 3,572, 5,828
Precinct 6 50%, 5,125
Totals 52,900, 25,177, 27,723
1. 52,900
2. 25,177
3. 27,723
4. 48%
5. 52%
6. Candidate B
7. Percents because it's faster to compare smaller numbers.

Life skill/page 143
1. $1440
2. $1305
3. $5220
4. $145
5. $469.80
6. $1409.40
7. $39.15
8. $184.15
9. $6629.40
10. $7934.40
11. 21.6%

Calculators/page 144
1. 4250
2. 61.74
3. 638.4
4. 7.045
5. 43.5% (rounded)

Calculators/page 145
1. Interest: $14.38
   Balance: $1014.38
2. Interest: $14.58
   Balance: $1028.96
3. Interest: $14.79
   Balance: $1043.75
4. Interest: $15.00
   Balance: $1058.75
5. Interest: $58.75
   Balance: $1058.75
6. Interest: $31.25
   Balance: $1031.25
7. Interest: $32.23
   Balance: $1063.48
8. Interest: $63.48
   Balance: $1063.48
6-month savings certificate at $6\frac{1}{4}\%$ offers the best interest rate.

Practice/page 146
1. $169.50
2. $20.00
3. 13.4%
4. $14.25
5. $5.75
6. $1449
7. $69
8. 5%
9. 5% of the sale price
10. no

Calculators/page 147
1. $.71, $47.87
2. $1.28, $86.80
3. $2.03, $137.43
4. $3.31, $223.95
5. $8.48, $573.75
6. $.17, $11.27

Life skill/page 148
1. Washer
   55%, $317.75
2. Dryer
   $70.30, $260.30
3. TV
   $300, $427.50
4. Freezer
   66.5%, $333.00
5. Microwave
   $108.00, $432.00
6. Range
   $250, $386.25
7. yes
8. Washer
   $25.42, 8%
9. Dryer
   $26.03, 10%
10. TV
   $29.07, 6.8%
11. Freezer
   $27.75, $8\frac{1}{3}\%$

12. Microwave
   $23.76, $5\frac{1}{2}\%$
13. Range
   $77.25, 20%

Practice/page 149
1. 80   9. 150
2. 55   10. 8
3. 3   11. 33
4. 42   12. 12
5. 40   13. 78
6. 12   14. 25
7. 63   15. 28
8. 10   16. 15

Calculators/page 150
1. 21,600   6. 44
2. 107.71   7. 1.11
3. 756   8. 114.8
4. .23   9. .10
5. .01   10. 540

Practice/page 151
1. clerical
2. 1,557,200
3. 8.9%
4. 258,400
5. 5,780,000

Life skill/page 152
1. millions
2. 17.6 million
3. 3.5 million
4. 14.1 million
5. 80%
6. $\frac{17}{14}$
7. 57%

Life skill/page 153
1. c
2. b
3. b
4. c

Practice/page 154
2. 4 yards 36 inches or 5 yards
3. 84 hours 315 minutes or 89 hours 15 minutes or $89\frac{1}{4}$ hours
4. 9 days 33 hours or 10 days 9 hours or $10\frac{3}{8}$ days
5. 30 miles 6600 feet or 31 miles 1320 feet or $31\frac{1}{4}$ miles
6. 2 yards 2 feet or $2\frac{2}{3}$ yards
7. 1 pound 6 ounces or $1\frac{3}{8}$ pounds

8. 4 gallons 2 quarts
    or $4\frac{1}{2}$ gallons
9. 1000 pounds
    or $\frac{1}{2}$ ton
10. 1 pint
11. 30 seconds
    or $\frac{1}{2}$ minute
12. 13 miles

Practice/page 155
1. 85 gallons 2 quarts
    or $85\frac{1}{2}$ gallons
2. 60 bushes
3. 42 pounds 2 ounces
4. 4 feet 7 inches
5. 8 gallons 3 quarts
    or $8\frac{3}{4}$ gallons
6. 500 pounds
7. 378 yards 2 feet
    or $378\frac{2}{3}$ yards

Life skill/page 156
1. 3 p.m.
2. 4:25 p.m.
3. 4 a.m.
4. 10:20 p.m.
5. 3

Life skill/page 157
1. $.02
    $.0225
    (Nose drops)
2. $.019
    $.02
    (Antiseptic)
3. $.125
    $.1375
    (Bandage tape)
4. $.03
    $.0325
    (Diaper rash cream)
5. $.005
    $.00375
    (Performer alcohol)
6. $.0225
    $.022
    (Tibb's Antacid)

Practice/page 158
2. .985 l
3. 40.36 kg
4. .85 km
5. 32.135 kg
6. 15.15 l
7. 40.15 m
8. .943 kg
9. 2.75 l
10. .6 m
11. 4.005 l
12. 60.012 kg

Life skill/page 159
1. 53.5 kg
2. 29 km
3. 6.75 l
4. 2.25 l
5. 1.25 m
6. 33 kg

Life skill/page 161
1. $7,975.00
2. $610.00
3. $253.23
4. $466.00
5. $6,645.77

Life skill/page 162
1. $9,235.00
2. $3,000.00
3. $6,235.00
4. $66.00
5. $661.00
6. $508.00
7. $153.00
8. $10,055.00
9. $4,000.00
10. $6,055.00
11. $495.00
12. $487.00
13. $8.00

Sample pre-employment test/pages 163, 164
1. c   6. b
2. a   7. b
3. c   8. a
4. d   9. b
5. a   10. c